MW01231529

JOHN C. MAXWELL
& CHRIS HODGES

JESUS
the HIGH
ROAD
LEADER

FOLLOW THE PATH HE
WANTS US TO TRAVEL

JESUS THE HIGH ROAD LEADER

Follow the Path He Wants Us To Travel

TABLE OF CONTENTS

ACKNOWLEDGMENTS

When we got the idea for this book, we immediately knew we wanted to get help from good leaders and friends who could help us identify the many ways Jesus took the high road with others. We want to thank the people who shared their knowledge and insights with us:

Sam Chand
Terence Chatmon
Tim Elmore
Daniel Floyd
Don Gibson
Jeff Henderson
Shaun Nepstad
John Nuzzo
Ike Reighard
Dan Reiland
Colleen Rouse
Chris Stephens
Greg Surratt
Dawn Yoder

In addition, John wants to thank Charlie Wetzel, Jared Cagle, Linda Eggers, and Erin Miller for their contributions to this book. Chris wants to thank Dudley Delffs.

HIGH ROAD LEADER
IN SANDALS OF GRACE

High road leader in sandals of grace,

Acknowledging humanness, tears on His face.

Doing what's right for reasons so pure,

Giving more than He took, love to assure.

Gathering people, the Good News to hear,

Placing them first, they came from far and near.

Forgiving so freely, He didn't keep score,

Valuing all people gave Him instant rapport.

Living a life so authentic and real,

Speaking words of great hope had such an appeal.

Sharing His message with love on His face,

High Road Leader in sandals of grace.

— JOHN C. MAXWELL

1

WHAT ROAD WILL YOU TAKE?

Jesus has a message for every one of his followers, a message that is clear and life changing. He expressed it in Matthew 5:13-16:

> [Jesus said,] "Let me tell you why you are here. You're here to be salt-seasoning that brings out the God-flavors of this earth. If you lose your saltiness, how will people taste godliness? You've lost your usefulness and will end up in the garbage."
>
> Here's another way to put it: "You're here to be light, bringing out the God-colors in the world. God is not a secret to be kept. We're going public with this, as public as a city on a hill. If I make you light-bearers, you don't think I'm going to hide you under a bucket, do you? I'm putting you on a light stand. Now that I've put you there on a hilltop, on a light stand—shine! Keep open house; be generous with your lives. By opening up to others, you'll prompt people to open up with God, this generous Father in heaven." (MSG)

Jesus wants us to be salt and light. Salt makes things better, and light makes things brighter. We are called to make a positive difference in the lives of others.

Jesus modeled this every day of his life on earth by being an example of a leader living on the high road. What do I mean by the high road? There are only three paths we can walk in life:

- **The Low Road:** People on this road selfishly take more than they give, and as a result, instead of making the world better and brighter, they make the world worse and darker.

- **The Middle Road:** People on this road focus on fairness and often keep score. They may not be aware of it, but they maintain the status quo, and nothing gets better or brighter.

- **The High Road:** People on this road follow Jesus' example. They give more than they take. They serve others out of love. They turn the other cheek instead of taking offense. Their lives reflect the behavior of Jesus. And because they do these things, they make the world better and brighter.

Many Christians believe they can take the middle road and be like Jesus, but that isn't true. Follow the life of Jesus in the

Gospels, and it becomes clear that He has shown us the path we are to walk: the high road. In fact, Jesus expressed his opinion about Christians who follow the middle road. He spoke about them to the church of Laodicea in Revelation 3:16-17:

> JESUS WANTS US TO BE SALT AND LIGHT. SALT MAKES THINGS BETTER, AND LIGHT MAKES THINGS BRIGHTER.

I know you inside and out, and find little to my liking. You're not cold, you're not hot—far better to be either cold or hot! You're stale. You're stagnant. You make me want to vomit. You brag, "I'm rich, I've got it made, I need nothing from anyone," oblivious that in fact you're a pitiful, blind beggar, threadbare and homeless. (MSG)

Jesus wants everyone to follow him wholeheartedly on the high road.

HIGH OR LOW?

Several years ago, it was popular for Christians to wear bracelets that said, "WWJD?"—What Would Jesus Do? Those letters were meant to be a daily reminder to think about what Jesus would do in any situation they faced. While that may have been a good question, Chris and I want to encourage you to DWJD!— Do What Jesus Did! Take the same high road Jesus did. Look at Jesus' example and follow it.

Jesus valued all people—do I value all people?

Jesus gave more than he received—do I give more than I receive?

Jesus didn't keep score—do I stop myself from keeping score?

Jesus acknowledged his humanness—do I acknowledge my humanness?

Jesus did the right things for the right reasons—do I do the right things for the right reasons?

Jesus lived an authentic life—do I live an authentic life?

Jesus placed others first—do I place others first?

Jesus brought people together—do I bring people together?

Jesus embraced God's values and lived them out perfectly. Contrast the life and leadership of Jesus with the people who are leading today. Our world is experiencing a values deficit. Too many leaders devalue people who are not like them and fail to live out high-road values. Sadly, this happens even in the Church. Why? I believe we have become distracted. Too many of us have put our hope in government and human laws to bring about a better life for us. Even worse, we put our hope in elected leaders of both parties who don't embrace the values of Jesus. Many of these people are low-road leaders who lack civility, lack authenticity, divide the people, place themselves and their party above everyone else, keep score, and get even with others when they lose. They have no idea how to be a servant leader.

Jesus modeled the way by washing people's feet and going to the cross. And he challenged his followers to make sacrifices to serve others, rather than expecting others to make sacrifices to serve them. He said, "Whoever wants to be my disciple must deny themselves and take up their cross daily and follow me. For whoever wants to save their life will lose it, but whoever loses their life for me will save it" (Luke 9:23-24).

Following the example of politics, we have allowed our *differences* with others to become *divisions* between ourselves and others. While differences are inevitable, creating divisions is a choice. It isn't necessary for us to build walls with others to follow Jesus' example. For example, my wife, Margaret, and I have been married for fifty-five years. There are areas where we do not agree, yet we still love, value, and respect each other.

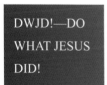

DWJD!—DO WHAT JESUS DID!

People will tell you to create divisions, pull away, or challenge the opposition. During an election season, they will say the most important decision you will make is who you vote for. That's not true. The most important decision is who you are going to *be*! Jesus said, "In the same way I loved you, you love one another.

> THE MOST IMPORTANT DECISION IS WHO YOU ARE GOING TO *BE*!

This is how everyone will recognize that you are my disciples—when they see the love you have for each other" (John 13:34-35, MSG). The modeling of Jesus the high-road leader and everything in Scripture calls all Christ followers to walk a higher road than others do.

HOW WILL YOU WALK?

Recently my pastor, Todd Mullins, challenged everyone in the congregation of Christ Fellowship to adopt a biblical perspective of who we are as Christians and how to live our lives. As he did this, he reminded us of three truths about ourselves as followers of Christ:

1. We Are Not Only Citizens of a Country—We Are Citizens of Heaven

In his letter to the Philippians, Paul challenged them not to be "enemies of the cross of Christ." He pointed out, "Their mind is set on earthly things," and reminded them as followers of Christ,

"But our citizenship is in heaven. And we eagerly await a Savior from there, the Lord Jesus Christ, who, by the power that enables him to bring everything under his control, will transform our lowly bodies so that they will be like his glorious body" (3:18-21). In other words, the world we inhabit is not our world. We are only passing through it, and we must never forget that.

2. We Are Not Just Citizens of Heaven—We are Ambassadors of Christ

To the people of Corinth, Paul stated that God "has committed to us the message of reconciliation. We are therefore Christ's ambassadors, as though God were making his appeal through us" (2 Corinthians 5:19-20). The role of an ambassador is an important one. Ambassadors represent their leader and their nation or kingdom in everything they say or do. As ambassadors for Christ and his Kingdom, we do not have the freedom of expressing our own message. Our message is that of reconciliation between God and people.

Jesus, our high-road leader, expects us to live out high-road behavior with others in everything we do. Our world is filled with people who live on the low road. That's understandable because our world is filled with sin and darkness. What kind of ambassadors are we if our actions and values as Christians are the same as those who have no relationship with God? When we live that way, how can we be a light in this dark world?

> AMBASSADORS REPRESENT THEIR LEADER AND THEIR NATION OR KINGDOM IN EVERYTHING THEY SAY OR DO. AS AMBASSADORS FOR CHRIST . . . OUR MESSAGE IS THAT OF RECONCILI-ATION BETWEEN GOD AND PEOPLE.

3. We Are Not Just Ambassadors of Christ—We are Chosen to Do Priestly Work

In his first epistle, the apostle Peter wrote to believers,

> But you are the ones chosen by God, chosen for the high calling of priestly work, chosen to be a holy people, God's instruments to do his work and speak out for him, to tell others of the night-and-day difference he made for you—from nothing to something, from rejected to accepted.

Friends, this world is not your home, so don't make yourselves cozy in it. Don't indulge your ego at the expense of your soul. Live an exemplary life in your neighborhood so that your actions will refute their prejudices. Then they'll be won over to God's side and be there to join in the celebration when he arrives. (1 Peter 2:9–12, MSG)

Our role as Christians is to help people connect with God. It's not possible to do that if we continually draw lines, argue with people, and build walls between us and them. Jesus came to this earth to be on common ground with us so he could connect us with God. As his chosen representatives, we must do the same.

When we take the high road, we love and value people the way Jesus did. That will make us look at people with whom we disagree in a different light. C. S. Lewis said, "There are no *ordinary* people. You have never talked to a mere mortal. . . . It is immortals whom we joke with, work with, marry, snub, and exploit."[1]

Knowing that Jesus took the high road with everyone, and knowing he wants you to follow his example, what are you going to do? Will you follow in his footsteps? Will you embrace *all* of Jesus' values? Your values are more than just decisions; they are your soul. The values you and I live determine how we behave and how our culture will function—regardless of the laws we make. Matters of the heart will never be solved with legislative action. It's much easier to rewrite the laws of the land than to change the heart. It's also less effective. Poet and critic Samuel Johnson was right when he wrote,

> "THERE ARE NO *ORDINARY* PEOPLE. YOU HAVE NEVER TALKED TO A MERE MORTAL."
> – C. S. LEWIS

How small of all that human hearts endure,
That part which laws or kings can cause or cure.[2]

As people who have been saved by grace, we know that only Jesus can cure the human heart. And that is the message we need to pass on to others. How can we best do that? By following Jesus, our high-road leader.

Chris and I have spent our lives striving to follow Jesus and share his message with others. Like you, we want to be salt and light so others will have a relationship with Jesus. To do that, we must make people hungry, not angry.

We want to share with you eight behaviors Jesus modeled in the Gospels that have taught and empowered us to be salt and light to others. Each of us explores four of them. We do this because only Jesus can make us attractive to people who don't know God. Only when we follow Jesus on the high road in a low-road world will people want to know why we're different. We want to lead people to Jesus. That only happens on the high road where Jesus travels.

2

JESUS VALUED ALL PEOPLE
John C. Maxwell

God is the original high-road leader. He loves and values people so much that anyone can have a whole and lasting life. He made that possible through Jesus. Here's how John the apostle expressed this truth:

> This is how much God loved the world: He gave his Son, his one and only Son. And this is why: so that no one need be destroyed; by believing in him, anyone can have a whole and lasting life. God didn't go to all the trouble of sending his Son merely to point an accusing finger, telling the world how bad it was. He came to help, to put the world right again.
> (John 3:16-17, MSG)

When John stated that God loved the world, he was making it clear that God loves and values *all people*. His desire is for

> WHEN JOHN STATED THAT GOD LOVED THE WORLD, HE WAS MAKING IT CLEAR THAT GOD LOVES AND VALUES *ALL PEOPLE.*

everyone to be saved, not to condemn them. Follow the footsteps of Jesus throughout the Gospels and you will conclude that Jesus valued everyone. We can become like Jesus when we follow his example of loving and valuing all people.

VALUING PEOPLE HELPS YOU SEE THEIR POTENTIAL

Jesus was always for the "outsiders." He was always looking for the one who was overlooked. He saw potential in those who seemingly had little to offer.

- Jesus looked at fishermen and believed they could be leaders.
- Jesus looked at Zacchaeus and believed he could become honest.
- Jesus looked at Lazarus and believed he could be raised.
- Jesus looked at the Samaritan woman and believed she had value.

- Jesus looked at the sick and believed they could be healed.
- Jesus looked at the thief and believed he could be forgiven.

Jesus saw people differently than others did. He looked beyond their problems and saw their potential. Most people see others as they are, with their shortcomings and sin. They ask, "Why do they behave like that?" Jesus looked beyond their problems and saw their possibilities. He asked, "How can I help them focus on their possibilities?"

This is what I know: God loves you more than you love yourself. He values you more than you value yourself. He also encourages you more than you encourage yourself. For anything negative that we can say to ourselves, God has a positive response for us:

You say: It's impossible.
God says: All things are possible (Luke 18:27).

You say: I'm too tired.
God says: I will give you rest (Matthew 11:28-30).

You say: Nobody really loves me.
God says: I love you (John 3:16).

You say: I can't go on.
God says: My grace is sufficient (2 Corinthians 12:9).

You say: I can't figure things out.
God says: I will direct your steps (Proverbs 3:5-6).

You say: I can't do it.
God says: You can do all things (Philippians 4:13).

You say: I'm not able.
God says: I am able (2 Corinthians 9:8).

You say: It's not worth it.
God says: I will be worth it (Romans 8:28).

You say: I can't forgive myself.
God says: I forgive you. (1 John 1:9 and Romans 8:1).

You say: I can't manage.
God says: I will supply all your needs (Philippians 4:19).

You say: I'm afraid.
God says: I have not given you a spirit of fear
              (2 Timothy 1:7).

You say: I'm always worried and frustrated.
God says: Cast all your cares on ME (1 Peter 5:7).

You say: I'm not smart enough.
God says: I give you wisdom (1 Corinthians 1:30).

You say: I feel all alone.
             God says: I will never leave you or forsake you
             (Hebrews 13:5).[3]

The life of Jesus the high-road leader offers hope to people. The Scriptures are filled with hope offered to people who have none. Why? Because Jesus loves us—all of us. As my friend Max Lucado says, "If God had a refrigerator, your picture would be on it."[4] God is crazy about you!

> THE LIFE OF JESUS THE HIGH-ROAD LEADER OFFERS HOPE TO PEOPLE.

HOW IMPORTANT IS VALUING EVERYONE?

When Jesus was asked what the greatest commandment is, he replied, "'Love the Lord your God with all your heart and with all your soul and with all your mind.' This is the first and greatest commandment. And the second is like it: 'Love your neighbor as yourself'" (Matthew 22:37-39). Jesus could not have spelled it out more simply: love God and love others. That's what he did and how he lived. And that's what he expects us to do also. To be like Jesus, we must live his good values and value the people he values. That means *everyone*.

Look at who Jesus brought together as his leaders, and you can see that he valued people from different backgrounds. Andrew and Peter were fishermen. James and John were not only fishermen, but also business owners who hired others to work for them (Mark 1:20). Matthew was a tax collector, a publican who was not considered worthy of tithing to the Temple. Simon was a zealot, a religious and political revolutionary. The other disciples were probably fishermen or tradesmen. Jesus' followers included beggars, women, Samaritans, prostitutes, Roman generals, Pharisees—people from all over Palestine and all walks of life. Jesus valued people in every situation: when he was developing his leaders, when he was ministering to the crowds, and in one-on-one interactions.

Jesus valued others based upon who he is, not who they were

or what they had done. No one had to be a friend or even good to be loved by Jesus. In fact, he said, "Love your enemies, do good to those who hate you, bless those who curse you, pray for those who mistreat you" (Luke 6:27-28). He valued and reached out to people others shunned or avoided, like the woman at the well, who was living in sin (John 4:7-30), and Zacchaeus, a

> JESUS VALUED OTHERS BASED UPON WHO HE IS, NOT WHO THEY WERE OR WHAT THEY HAD DONE.

despised tax collector (Luke 19:1-10). Even as he suffered on the cross, he valued and forgave the repentant criminal on the cross next to him (Luke 23:40-43). And he taught reconciliation. Luke 5:31-32 describes how Jesus defended eating with tax collectors when the Pharisees and teachers of the law criticized him for spending time with sinners.

Look at how Jesus saw people and valued them:

Jesus Saw More in People Than Their Past

As a high-road leader, Jesus assumed the best in people and treated them with love and respect. Here's what happened when he met a man named Matthew who had cheated people in the past as a tax collector:

As Jesus went on from there, he saw a man named Matthew sitting at the tax collector's booth. "Follow me," he told him, and Matthew got up and followed him. While Jesus was having dinner at Matthew's house, many tax collectors and sinners came and ate with him and his disciples. When the Pharisees saw this, they asked his disciples, "Why does your teacher eat with tax collectors and sinners?" On hearing this, Jesus said, "It is not the healthy who need a doctor, but the sick. But go and learn what this means: 'I desire mercy, not sacrifice.' For I have not come to call the righteous, but sinners." (Matthew 9:9-13)

In essence, Jesus said, "You'd make a great addition to my team."

Jesus saw the bigger picture of what Matthew's life could be when others couldn't. This occurred continually when Jesus looked at people. He saw potential in "unschooled, ordinary men" and made them catalytic leaders of world change. How? They "had been with Jesus" (Acts 4:13). What is the value lesson we can take away from this? *Knowing that Jesus values us increases our self-worth and brings the best out of us.*

Jesus Saw More in People Than Their Status

Luke recounts a discussion about the greatest commandment between Jesus and an expert in the law. Hoping to narrow down the list of who he might be expected to love, the expert asked

Jesus to define who he meant by *neighbor*. Here's what happened:

> In reply Jesus said: "A man was going down from
> Jerusalem to Jericho, when he was attacked by robbers.
> They stripped him of his clothes, beat him and went
> away, leaving him half dead. A priest happened to be
> going down the same road, and when he saw the man,
> he passed by on the other side. So too, a Levite, when he
> came to the place and saw him, passed by on the other
> side. But a Samaritan, as he traveled, came where the man
> was; and when he saw him, he took pity on him. He went
> to him and bandaged his wounds, pouring on oil and
> wine. Then he put the man on his own donkey, brought
> him to an inn and took care of him. The next day he took
> out two denarii and gave them to the innkeeper. 'Look
> after him,' he said, 'and when I return, I will reimburse
> you for any extra expense you may have.'
>
> "Which of these three do you think was a neighbor
> to the man who fell into the hands of robbers?"
>
> The expert in the law replied, "The one who had
> mercy on him." Jesus told him, "Go and do likewise."
> (Luke 10:30-37)

Why did Jesus choose to illustrate this story using a
Samaritan? Because his Jewish audience would have seen the
Samaritan as a political, spiritual, and racial enemy—someone
despised. Jesus, in contrast, saw him as someone of value. And

Jesus wanted his followers to be like him. We are to go out of our way and pay a price for others, like the Good Samaritan. In other words, we are to find people who are beat up, who've fallen, who are broken, and we are to restore them.

Jesus gave his life to restore us, and he gave this example to encourage us to restore others. We will do that only if we value them.

> You won't restore an old car unless you see value in it.
> You won't restore a piece of furniture unless you see
>   value in it.
> You won't restore people unless you see value in them.

Do you see value in everyone the way Jesus does?

Recently I was speaking about valuing people to a non-religious audience. During Q & A, a lady asked, "How can you say you value me when you don't know me?" That's a perfectly logical question from someone who doesn't know God. But it's a question we as followers of Christ should know the answer to. We value people because God values them. He created each person and values them greatly. Therefore, even though we may not know someone, we value them because he values them. That not only makes us more like Jesus, it gives us the best opportunity of introducing others to Jesus.

What is the value lesson we can learn from this? *My perspective of others determines my behavior toward them, and my behavior toward them influences their response to me.*

Jesus Saw More in People Than Their Sin

The religious leaders of Jesus' day wanted to devalue and discredit him, and they tried to push him to treat others similarly. But Jesus wouldn't do it. Instead, he took the high road:

> The teachers of the law and the Pharisees brought in a woman caught in adultery. They made her stand before the group and said to Jesus, "Teacher, this woman was caught in the act of adultery. In the Law Moses commanded us to stone such women. Now what do you say?" They were using this question as a trap, in order to have a basis for accusing him.
>
> But Jesus bent down and started to write on the ground with his finger. When they kept on questioning him, he straightened up and said to them, "Let any one of you who is without sin be the first to throw a stone at her." Again he stooped down and wrote on the ground.
>
> At this, those who heard began to go away one at a time, the older ones first, until only Jesus was left, with the woman still standing there. Jesus straightened up and asked her, "Woman, where are they? Has no one condemned you?"
>
> "No one, sir," she said.

"Then neither do I condemn you," Jesus declared. "Go now and leave your life of sin."
(John 8:3-11)

When Jesus addressed her as "woman," he spoke the same word he used when he was on the cross and said to Mary, "Woman, behold your son." He wasn't accusing her; he was calling her a woman of great value. She was guilty, and the religious people devalued her. While they were writing her off, Jesus was showing her how to write a new story with her life. Jesus used his authority to liberate rather than condemn her. Forgiving her and challenging her to change, he removed her fear and gave her a new path to follow.

I wish we were more like Jesus. We live in a world with people like the ones described in an illustration I read many years ago called "The Pit." Here's what it said:

A man fell into a pit and couldn't get himself out.
A SUBJECTIVE person came along and said:
   "I FEEL for you, down there."
An OBJECTIVE person said:
   "It's logical that someone would fall down there."
A CHRISTIAN SCIENTIST came along:
   "You only THINK you are in a pit."

A PHARISEE said:

"Only BAD people fall into a pit."

A MATHEMATICIAN

calculated HOW he fell into the pit.

A ROCK-HOUND

asked him of any rare specimens in the pit.

A NEWS-REPORTER

wanted the exclusive story on his pit.

A FUNDAMENTALIST said:

"You DESERVE your pit. . . ."

A REALIST said:

"That's a pit. . . . "

A GEOLOGIST

told him to appreciate the rock strata in the pit.

An I.R.S. man

asked if he was paying taxes on the pit.

The COUNTY INSPECTOR

asked if he had a permit to dig a pit.

A PROFESSOR

gave him a lecture on: *The Elementary Principles of the Pit.*

An EVASIVE person:

avoided the subject of the pit altogether.

A SELF-PITYING person said:

"You haven't seen anything until you've

seen **MY PIT!! . . .**"

A CHARISMATIC said:

"Just CONFESS that you're not in a pit."

AN OPTIMIST said:

"Things COULD be worse."

A PESSIMIST said:

"Things WILL get worse!!"

JESUS, seeing the man, took him by the hand and LIFTED HIM OUT of the pit.[5]

AS JESUS' FOLLOWERS AND AMBASSADORS, WE NEED TO VALUE EVERYONE ENOUGH TO REACH OUT TO THEM WHEN THEY FALL AND LIFT THEM BACK UP AGAIN.

As Jesus' followers and ambassadors, we need to value everyone enough to reach out to them when they fall and lift them back up again. What is the value lesson we can learn from this? *See past others' sins and see the value Jesus sees in them.*

FOLLOWING IN JESUS' FOOTSTEPS

When I think about Jesus and I read about how he loved people, it prompts me to ask myself, "Am I like Jesus? Am I valuing others in a way that gives them hope?" The apostle Peter said, "Always be prepared to give the reason for the hope that you have. But do this with gentleness and respect" (1 Peter 3:15). Am I doing that?

I know I haven't always followed Jesus' example. Despite knowing who Jesus was and what he did since I was a boy, it took me years to follow in Jesus' footsteps. The first example I had of how Jesus walked was my father. Dad loved people. As a leader he walked slowly through the crowd, listening to and encouraging people. When he was ninety, he said to me, "John, isn't it wonderful that as we get older, we love people more?" My answer was, "Dad, that is true of you because you have always loved people!" He grew to love others more because he first made the decision to love all people.

I benefited from Dad's example, but I remember the day I made the conscious choice to try to love people the way Jesus did. It was on the day I graduated from college. At dinner, I asked Dad to give me his best advice as I started my career as a pastor. He said, "John, every day believe in people, value people, and unconditionally love them. If you do these three things every day, you will be a leader people want to follow." He was right.

For over fifty-five years I have strived to live out that advice, and I have received the blessings of his words.

I led churches as a pastor from 1969 to 1995, and throughout those years my greatest passion was sharing my faith. I also led conferences and wrote books to equip pastors to become better leaders. In 1993, when my publisher told me more of my books were selling to a general audience than to Christians, I was surprised. That knowledge started to stir something inside of me. I was reminded of Paul's words: "I entered their world and tried to experience things from their point of view" (1 Corinthians 9:19, MSG). I soon felt a calling to cross over to the secular world so that I could be salt and light to people outside the church. Two years later, I resigned from the pastorate and changed my primary audience.

THE CLOSER I GOT TO LOST PEOPLE, THE MORE I LOVED THEM. AND THE MORE I LOVED THEM, THE MORE RECEPTIVE THEY BECAME TO HEARING ABOUT MY FAITH.

Entering this other world was life changing to me. For twenty-six years I had been surrounded by the church community. Suddenly, I was the outsider. I needed to listen to and learn from lost people so I could connect with them. I never lost my identity in Christ, but I did gain a greater passion for people far from God. I felt I better understood his love for the world, and that brought me closer to him. The closer I got to people without a relationship with God, the more I loved them. And the more I loved them, the more receptive they became to hearing about my faith. The principle we can learn from this is very simple: *Valuing all people opens the door for relationships with them and offers opportunities to share our faith.* That's why Jesus said, "By opening up to others, you'll prompt people to open up with God" (Matthew 5:16, MSG).

TIME WITH LOST SHEEP

If we as Christians separate ourselves from lost people, we become more likely to judge them. We need to remember that God doesn't ask us to change before he'll accept us. He accepts us so he can change

> GOD DOESN'T ASK US TO CHANGE BEFORE HE'LL ACCEPT US. HE ACCEPTS US SO HE CAN CHANGE US!

us! Accepting people where they are creates a common ground, and the road between others and Jesus is common ground, not a battle ground.

When I speak to Christian audiences, to remind them of Jesus' love for people, I lead them through an exercise. I tell them, "Say to the person beside you, 'Jesus loves and values you.'" They gladly do so. Then I say, "Tell the person beside you that Jesus loves and values *me*." They respond even more enthusiastically because they like being reminded how much Jesus loves them. "Tell them, 'Jesus loves and values people I don't know,'" I say, and they do. At this point, people are smiling, and we're all having a great time. Then I say, "Tell them, 'Jesus loves and values people I don't like,'" and that's when they stumble. Some people get the words out awkwardly, being reminded that God loves *everyone*. Others simply look dumbstruck, realizing they have been devaluing people that God values.

Our behavior toward others often determines their behavior towards us—and toward our faith. How are you treating others? Are you separating yourself from them? Are you building walls? Instead, find a gate and develop a relationship. Jesus said, "Shine! Keep open house; be generous with your lives" (Matthew 5:16, MSG). You may be the door that either opens or closes the way to God for a lost person. Value people and open the door to them so that your light shines on them.

Everything Jesus did with others was relational. He said,

Are you tired? Worn out? Burned out on religion? Come to me. Get away with me and you'll recover your life. I'll show you how to take a real rest. Walk with me and work with me—watch how I do it. Learn the unforced rhythms of grace. I won't lay anything heavy

or ill-fitting on you. Keep company with me and you'll learn to live freely and lightly.
(Matthew 11:28-30, MSG)

Every part of his invitation to lost people was relational. You can see it in his words: "Come to me . . . I'll show you how . . . Walk with me . . . Work with me . . . Watch how I do it . . . Keep company with me."

Jesus' invitation to the lost is the same for you and me. Jesus wants you to walk with him. He wants you to work with him. He wants you to watch him. Will you? Will you choose to travel the high road by valuing all people as he did? Will you connect with lost people instead of trying to correct them when Jesus didn't ask you to? Will you be the salt and light Jesus asked us to become, making your faith attractive to others? We know you can. We hope you will.

3

JESUS GAVE MORE THAN HE TOOK

Chris Hodges

Giving more than you take is at the core of taking the high road and being a servant leader. When you give more than you take, you exemplify the very nature of Jesus. This value provides the soil in which all the other high-road values grow and flourish, yielding a heart that gives and a hand that is open.

You can see this in the very first miracle performed at a wedding in Cana. The wine ran out—a terrible embarrassment for the bride and groom, along with their families. So Jesus intervened and blessed those who would otherwise have been embarrassed. When Jesus turned water into wine, though, he did more than perform a miracle—he revealed his high-road nature as the Son of God who gives more than he takes. The place where people went to party, to enjoy the best food and drink provided by the hosts, became the setting where Jesus gave with divine generosity.

The way Jesus consistently gave more than he took

demonstrated his unconditional love, the same love displayed by his Father in sending Jesus. This is clear in one of the most familiar explanations of the gospel: "For God so loved the world that he *gave* his one and only Son" (John 3:16, emphasis added).

The very path of Jesus is the model for your calling as a high-road leader, the call to get past yourself for the sake of those you serve through your leadership. God's Word urges, "Do nothing out of selfish ambition or vain conceit. Rather, in humility value others above yourselves, not looking to your own interests but each of you to the interests of others" (Philippians 2:3-4). Jesus provided the context for this way of thinking when he said, "So the last will be first, and the first will be last" (Matthew 20:16).

Probably the most profound teaching about "giving more than you take," though, isn't found in the Gospels. It's summed up by the apostle Paul when he urged us to remember the words of Jesus himself, "It is more blessed to give than to receive" (Acts 20:35). The word translated here as *blessed* comes from the Greek word *makarios*, which literally means "happy in the soul."

> "IT IS MORE BLESSED TO GIVE THAN TO RECEIVE."
> —JESUS

This meaning is also a reminder that the opposite of generosity is misery. The word *misery* comes from the word *miser,* one who is stingy and unwilling to give at all. Think of Scrooge at the beginning of *A Christmas Carol* and the miserly attitude of his heart that motivated his terrible treatment of everyone around him. By the end of his Christmas Eve journey, Scrooge realized the personal and relational cost of clinging to his wealth.

Something good gets released inside of you when you give. Letting go of the need to be self-sufficient, to hold on to what you've been entrusted to steward, eradicates misery from your life. You discover the joy that comes with being a blessing. As *The Message* puts it, "You'll not likely go wrong here if you keep remembering that our Master said, 'You're far happier giving than getting'" (Acts 20:35).

GENEROSITY IS CONTAGIOUS

The value of your life isn't determined by how much you achieve or accumulate but by how much of your life you give away. Winston Churchill understood this truth when he said, "We make a living by what we get, but we make a life by what we give." That's why the Bible encourages us to give more than we take. This kind of generosity not only stores up treasures in heaven, but also gives us the life that is truly abundant, full, and blessed. The apostle Paul wrote, "Command them to do good, to be rich in good deeds, and to be generous and willing to share. In this way they will lay up treasure for themselves as a firm foundation for the coming age, so that they may take hold of the life that is truly life" (1 Timothy 6:18-19).

One of the best stories to illustrate the way Jesus gave more than he took occurred when Jesus washed the feet of the disciples. On the night before he would be crucified, Jesus focused on giving to his followers in a way that would show them how to lead by serving. It's important to note that this is the only time in Scripture when Jesus explicitly tells us, "I have given you an example to follow. Do as I have done to you" (John 13:15, NLT). As the ultimate high-road leader, Jesus emphasized how essential it is to give, making servanthood both the motive and method for leadership.

We might be tempted to think, *It was so easy for Jesus to give more than take—after all, he's the Son of God,* but this incredible scene of humility shows Jesus' willingness to put others first even in the midst of his own needs. You know he was carrying the pressure and weight of taking on the whole world's sins. That meant he had tremendous needs of his own—but he still gave to his disciples at that time *and* gave us an example that remains timeless. John recounted what happened:

> It was just before the Passover Festival. Jesus knew that the hour had come for him to leave this world and go to the Father. Having loved his own who were in the world, he loved them to the end.
>
> The evening meal was in progress, and the devil had already prompted Judas, the son of Simon Iscariot, to betray

Jesus. Jesus knew that the Father had put all things under his power, and that he had come from God and was returning to God; so he got up from the meal, took off his outer clothing, and wrapped a towel around his waist. After that, he poured water into a basin and began to wash his disciples' feet, drying them with the towel that was wrapped around him.

He came to Simon Peter, who said to him, "Lord, are you going to wash my feet?"

Jesus replied, "You do not realize now what I am doing, but later you will understand."

"No," said Peter, "you shall never wash my feet."

Jesus answered, "Unless I wash you, you have no part with me."

"Then, Lord," Simon Peter replied, "not just my feet but my hands and my head as well!"

Jesus answered, "Those who have had a bath need only to wash their feet; their whole body is clean. And you are clean, though not every one of you." For he knew who was going to betray him, and that was why he said not every one was clean.

When he had finished washing their feet, he put on his clothes and returned to his place. "Do you understand what I have done for you?" he asked them. "You call me 'Teacher' and 'Lord,' and rightly so, for that is what I am. Now that I, your Lord and Teacher, have washed your feet, you also should wash one another's feet. I have set you an example that you should do as I have done for you. Very truly I tell you, no servant is greater than his master, nor is a messenger greater than the one who sent him. Now that you know these things, you will be blessed if you do them. (John 13:1-17)

Reading this account of Jesus' actions, I observe,

- He gave because he knew who he was.
- He gave freely in love because of his identity and purpose.
- He gave even though Peter misunderstood his gift.
- He gave even though he knew Judas was going to betray him.

GENEROSITY IS SPIRITUALLY CONTAGIOUS. "YOU HAVE BEEN TREATED GENEROUSLY, SO LIVE GENEROUSLY." MATTHEW 10:8

Tremendous freedom comes from knowing who we are and what we are called to do. Seeing Jesus' example and how generous he was, we should be inspired to emulate him.

GOD THE ULTIMATE GIVER

Our heavenly Father modeled unfathomable generosity by giving his first and best when he gave his Son Jesus to us. That generosity does something in us. When we experience the limitless love and grace of Christ, we want to live out what we have been given and extend to others the same gift, the same opportunity to know the goodness and mercy of God. Generosity is spiritually contagious. "You have been *treated generously*, so *live generously*" (Matthew 10:8, MSG, emphasis added).

> "IF ONE FIRST GIVES HIMSELF TO THE LORD, ALL OTHER GIVING IS EASY."
> —JOHN BONNELL

When I first became a Christian, I was told I should give some of my resources back to God. Being young and innocent, I didn't question or resist it. I figured, *if that's what God asks of me, then I'm happy to do it as part of my new identity*. I never saw it as optional or obligatory—it was just essential and joyful. As John S. Bonnell said, "If one first gives himself to the Lord, all other giving is easy."[6] Over the years as God has continued to bless me and entrust more to me, I have tried to expand my capacity for generosity and consistently increase my giving.

Throughout the Bible, God asks his people to be givers. We are to return a portion of our income to him from our firstfruits and to offer more as we grow in the gift of giving. I love giving because it identifies me in some small way with our great God. Everything about the nature of God is giving.

In sharp contrast to the Lord's abundant giving, everything about the nature of the devil is taking. Givers think only of what's in it for the other person, while takers only think of what's in it for themselves. Simply put, a sacrifice will always cost you something, while selfishness will always look to gain something.

We see this stark contrast in an incident involving a very expensive gift offered to Jesus—a luxurious perfume used by a woman to wash Jesus' feet. Jesus received her lavish generosity even while those at the dinner party around him, including his own disciple Judas Iscariot, expressed contempt and concern. This event depicts one of the greatest expressions of love ever shown to Jesus and is one of the few scenes recorded in all four Gospels: Matthew 26:6-13; Mark 14:3-9; Luke 7:36-50; and John 12:1-8.

Jesus was eating at someone's house when a woman who was known to be a sinner poured expensive perfume on Jesus' feet, weeping over them and drying them with her hair. Her bold display created quite an issue with the spectators, who reacted in anger to that kind of woman being in their midst and the cost of the luxurious perfume. Judas asked, "Why wasn't this perfume sold and the money given to the poor? It was worth a year's wages" (John 12:5).

To make sure we understand Judas's motive, John said Judas

wasn't concerned about the poor; he was the keeper of the money bag and liked to help himself from it (John 12:6). The sad reality is that Judas's attempt to discredit the woman and to profit himself backfired. This woman is forever remembered as the one who gave Jesus the last act of love before his death. Judas is forever remembered as the one who betrayed Jesus and brought the authorities to arrest him.

Looking at the contrast between the two of them, it's evident you can't give what you haven't received. You can't express what you haven't experienced yourself. Jesus explained, "Therefore, I tell you, her many sins have been forgiven—as her great love has shown. But he who has been forgiven little loves little" (Luke 7:47). Our capacity for love gets expanded as we receive the love of God. We love because he first loved us (1 John 4:19).

EVERYONE IS YOUR NEIGHBOR

To be a high-road leader like Jesus, you must give more than you take, being open-handed and open-hearted. This quality also affects the way you see other people and your willingness to love them despite your differences. John already discussed the parable of the Good Samaritan in chapter 2. Jesus told that story not only to teach the importance of helping someone, but also to encourage his listeners to go out of their way to be generous and show kindness and care to a stranger in need. The story reveals the way people tend to respond to those they encounter. And how we see people is how we'll treat people.

The thieves saw a victim to exploit. You may not be a robber, but sometimes we treat people the way these robbers did this traveler. We expect others to serve us and bend to our way of doing things. We use them, along with their resources and contributions, to fulfill our own self-enhancing agenda. In essence we assume, "What's yours is mine, and I'm going to take it."

The priest and Levite saw a problem to avoid. They were too busy doing self-righteous work to stop and give to someone in dire need. Sometimes we can be just as indifferent. We justify not having time or money to help someone suffering right in front of us. We assume others will help them, and we tell ourselves, "What's mine is mine, and I'm going to keep it."

The Good Samaritan saw a person to be loved. He was willing to give his time, attention, money, care, and compassion to a stranger left for dead and ignored by others. He saw this traveler in need as a fellow human being, someone deserving of his help. So he gave this wounded man all he could and expected nothing in return. His attitude was "What's mine is yours, and I'm to give it to you."

> ONE OF THE GREATEST REVELATIONS ABOUT YOUR LIFE IS THAT WHEN YOU FOLLOW JESUS, YOUR LIFE IS NOT YOUR OWN.

One of the greatest revelations about your life is that when you follow Jesus, your life is not your own. You have been bought with a price. And you should see others as people to be loved because you have been so graciously and mercifully forgiven and loved by God. Giving more than you take begins with how you see others.

WATERING CAMELS

While Jesus certainly gave more than he took, we might assume it was easy for him because he's the Son of God. But living as a man during his time on earth, Jesus also inherited an ancestral legacy of giving that went all the way back to his great-grandmother, to Rebekah, the wife of Isaac and mother of Jacob. Her story demonstrates the impact of giving more than you take.

Genesis says that Abraham was getting old and wanted a good wife for his son, Isaac, so Abraham sent his chief servant to go and find one. Abraham didn't want Isaac, his only child, leaving home and possibly making the wrong selection.

Abraham's servant left with ten camels and all kinds of items to use in making a deal. Feeling the pressure of finding a woman worthy of his master's son and wondering how he would know when he had, the servant prayed for a sign when he arrived at a well.

> Then he prayed, "LORD, God of my master Abraham, make me successful today, and show kindness to my master Abraham. See, I am standing beside this spring, and the daughters of the townspeople are coming out to draw water. May it be that when I say to a young woman, 'Please let down your jar that I may have a drink,' and she says, 'Drink, and I'll water your camels too'—let her be the one you have chosen for your servant Isaac. By this I will know that you have shown kindness to my master."
> (Genesis 24:12-14)

This was quite a bold prayer. You see, camels drink, on average, around twenty gallons of water at the end of a long hot day of traveling. The servant had ten camels—so if a young woman offered not only to get a drink for him but to water his camels, that was going way beyond what anyone would typically offer.

Sure enough, "Before he had finished praying, Rebekah came out with her jar on her shoulder" (Genesis 24:15). The servant asked her for a drink of water, and she agreed and said she would water his camels as well. Ten camels drinking about twenty gallons each equals two hundred gallons. This vast amount of water drawn with a five-gallon jar would require about forty trips to the well!

Only after Rebekah demonstrated a giving spirit with no-strings kindness did she discover the servant's mission. She expected nothing in return but was offered gold jewelry and a new husband. She had no idea how her act of generosity would change the rest of her life—and the lives of generations after her. That just goes to show, you never know what might happen when you water someone's camels. But that's not why you do it—you water them to serve, to give more than you take.

GIVING STARTS IN THE HEART

Because he possessed a heart to give, Jesus was willing to wash the dirty, dusty feet of his disciples—even those of Judas who would betray him that very night. Because Rebekah's spirit was right, she was willing to give more than was asked of her without expecting anything in return. Their examples remind us that giving more than you take begins with an attitude of generosity. That is the baseline, not a future goal. We might be tempted to say, "If I won the lottery, then I could afford to be generous," or "If I were retired, then I could afford to volunteer more of my time." High-road leaders who give more than they take start with what they have—not what they might have someday.

Jesus, as well as his thirty-seven-times-great-grandmother, was

HIGH-ROAD
LEADERS WHO
GIVE MORE THAN
THEY TAKE START
WITH WHAT THEY
HAVE—NOT WHAT
THEY MIGHT
HAVE SOMEDAY.

willing to do something menial, something humbling and tiring, without complaint. Rather than isolated acts, washing feet and watering camels reflected their character, their convictions, their core compassion. These acts exemplify high-road leadership in action.

Giving more than you take starts with the attitude of your heart, not the list of charities you support or the number of zeros in your donations. Every day you can give your attention, your interest, your compassion, and your wisdom to those around you. You can focus on investing in eternal intangibles rather than temporary possessions. You can follow the teaching of Jesus, who said, "Do not store up for yourselves treasures on earth, where moths and vermin destroy, and where thieves break in and steal. But store up for yourselves treasures in heaven, where moths and vermin do not destroy, and where thieves do not break in and steal" (Matthew 6:19-20). He was not saying that earthly treasure is wrong or bad—but that it simply will not last or hold value. The impact of your generosity, however, will outlive you.

You never know the effect an act of kindness can have for

someone else. Jesus said, "And if anyone gives even a cup of cold water to one of these little ones who is my disciple, truly I tell you, that person will certainly not lose their reward" (Matthew 10:42). High-road leaders know that small acts of giving reap big rewards. They know that encouraging texts, emails, and phone calls can bless others. They know that going above and beyond sets an example for everyone they're leading.

Giving more than you take now also has a huge impact on the lives of others in the future. Jesus said, "I sent you to reap what you have not worked for. Others have done the hard work, and you have reaped the benefits of their labor" (John 4:38). You and I have benefited from the willingness of countless others who give more than they take. To humble themselves and to serve. To steward their blessings in order to be a blessing to others.

High-road leaders give more than they take, knowing the example they set can ignite others to give more of themselves. This kind of giving is the ultimate in paying it forward. When you give like Jesus, you trust that your generosity will impact others for good.

SECOND-MILE GIVING

Jesus did more than demonstrate the value of giving through his example. He also instructed on this principle in his teaching. In the Sermon on the Mount, he emphasized the importance of not only giving more than you take, but of giving more than others expect:

> You have heard that it was said, "Eye for eye, and tooth for tooth." But I tell you, do not resist an evil person. If anyone slaps you on the right cheek, turn to them the other cheek also. And if anyone wants to sue you and take your shirt, hand over your coat as well.
>
> If anyone forces you to go one mile, go with them two miles. Give to the one who asks you, and do not turn away from the one who wants to borrow from you. (Matthew 5:38-42)

Citing the Old Testament law of "eye for eye," Jesus turned our human understanding of fairness on its head by asking them to do what is probably counter-intuitive for people. He challenged people to do more than is required of them when everyone naturally wants to do the least. He wanted us to do what was needed to get along with others and treat them like we want to be treated.

What if others are not willing to treat us with the kindness we extend to them? you may wonder. *What if they ask for more than we feel obligated to give?* Jesus said to overwhelm them with generosity, to surprise them by exceeding their request. If they say they're entitled to your shirt, give them your shirt and your coat, too. If someone forces you to walk a mile and carry a heavy pack and armor the way Roman soldiers often conscripted citizens to do, then carry their burden not just one mile but two.

Jesus, the ultimate high-road leader, taught that giving more than you take attracts others' attention. High-road leaders stand out because they go beyond what's required of them. They don't stand out when they do the bare minimum. They stand out because they give more than is reasonably expected. Jesus didn't say that the one who punches the best or hits the hardest wins the fight. No, he said to turn the other cheek.

What will set you and me apart from the rest of the world is the other cheek and the second mile. Jesus asks us to give more than what's expected. He didn't ask you to treat others fairly. Jesus told us to take the high road and to give more, care more, do more than anyone would ever expect. Why? Because our actions say, "I'm doing this first mile for you, but this second mile is only because of Jesus. When I go the second mile, you are going to see the Jesus in me." The second mile is where others feel it as well as see it.

As followers of Christ, we should always be looking for ways to go the second mile, even before others are considering going the first. In the face of adversity, we should *be kind* instead of treating

> JESUS TOLD US TO TAKE THE HIGH ROAD AND TO GIVE MORE, CARE MORE, DO MORE THAN ANYONE WOULD EVER EXPECT.

people *in kind*. When we do these things, we're being like Jesus, who went far beyond the second mile or any human measure in what he gave us. He gave his life so that everyone could be restored in relationship with his Father. Jesus not only told his followers, "Greater love has no one than this: to lay down one's life for one's friends" (John 15:13). He actually did it. He demonstrated his love by laying down his life for you and me and everyone else. He set the example of being a high-road leader who gives more than he takes.

Never forget that when we give, we give to the Lord and have the privilege of reflecting who God is—the ultimate giver. That is what Jesus expect us to do, and it is what we should strive to do every day.

4

JESUS DIDN'T KEEP SCORE
John C. Maxwell

People who travel on the low and middle roads of life keep score, and as a result, they damage relationships because they make their interactions with others transactional. They continually compare themselves to others in an effort to put themselves in a more favorable light. They keep count of all the times they give to someone or do good for them, and they count all the times that person takes or causes offense. When the score becomes too lopsided, the relationship typically tumbles and comes to an end. By its nature, keeping score is competitive. People do it to show themselves to be the winner and others the losers. Scorekeeping may be good for games—but not for relationships. That's why Jesus did not keep score.

If anyone had the right to keep score, it was Jesus. He is God in human flesh—the perfect man who never sinned. But he took the high road and used a different kind of math. No matter how many offenses

> SCOREKEEPING MAY BE GOOD FOR GAMES —BUT NOT FOR RELATIONSHIPS.

we have given him or what kind of negative score we have racked up, when we ask Jesus to forgive us, he wipes the slate clean. He has always loved without correction, given without expectation, and forgiven without condition.

Follow Jesus through the Gospels and you find him refusing to keep score and encouraging others to follow his example. While others despised and shunned Matthew, Jesus called him to be one of his disciples (Matthew 9:9). After miraculously restoring the sight of two blind men, Jesus told them not to tell anyone (Matthew 9:30). He didn't condemn the woman caught in adultery, but instead exhorted her to leave her life of sin (John 8:10-11). He emphasized forgiveness over judgment when a sinful woman anointed his feet (Luke 7:36-50). He taught the importance of forgiving others instead of keeping score in the parable of the unmerciful servant (Matthew 18:21-35). And he forgave his executioners (Luke 23:33-34).

Even Jesus' last act before his death on the cross was a high-road action showing that he did not keep score. As Jesus suffered between two criminals, the man on one side of him hurled insults. The one on the other side rebuked him:

> "Don't you fear God? . . . We are punished justly, for we are getting what our deeds deserve. But this man has done nothing wrong."
>
> Then he said, "Jesus, remember me when you come into your kingdom." Jesus answered him, "Truly I

tell you, today you will be with me in paradise."
(Luke 23:40-43)

Jesus didn't keep score because he saw a bigger picture. He took a different path, the same one we are encouraged to take as we run the race of our lives. The writer of Hebrews said followers of Christ should be "looking unto Jesus the author and finisher of our faith; who for the joy that was set before him endured the cross, despising the shame, and is set down at the right hand of the throne of God" (12:2, KJV). Instead of keeping score against the condemned man beside him, Jesus despised the shame, endured the cross, and forgave the sins of one who could never do anything to change the score for himself.

JESUS CHOSE TO KEEP FORGIVING

If you ever doubt the lengths to which Jesus was willing to go to avoid keeping score, you need to look no further than his interactions with Peter, the person to whom he would hand the keys of the kingdom of heaven (Matthew 16:19).

Peter was arrogant, and he kept score. He believed he was better than his fellow disciples, and he wasn't afraid to say so. On the night Jesus was to be arrested, Matthew recorded Peter's interaction with Jesus:

Then Jesus told them, "This very night you will all fall
away on account of me, for it is written:

> "'I will strike the shepherd, and the sheep of the
> flock will be scattered.'

But after I have risen, I will go ahead of you into
Galilee."

Peter replied, *"Even if all fall away on account of you,
I never will."*

"Truly I tell you," Jesus answered, "this very night,
before the rooster crows, you will disown me three
times."

But Peter declared, *"Even if I have to die with you, I
will never disown you."* And all the other disciples said
the same.

(Matthew 26:31-35, emphasis added)

But as Jesus knew would happen, Peter did not choose to die
with him. He didn't even stand up for Jesus or speak on his
behalf:

Now Peter was sitting out in the courtyard, and a
servant girl came to him. "You also were with Jesus of
Galilee," she said.

But *he denied it* before them all. "I don't know what
you're talking about," he said.

Then he went out to the gateway, where another

servant girl saw him and said to the people there, "This fellow was with Jesus of Nazareth."

He *denied it again, with an oath*: "I don't know the man!"

After a little while, those standing there went up to Peter and said, "Surely you are one of them; your accent gives you away."

Then he began to *call down curses, and he swore to them, "I don't know the man!"*

Immediately a rooster crowed. Then Peter remembered the word Jesus had spoken: "Before the rooster crows, *you will disown me three times*." And he went outside and *wept bitterly*.

(Matthew 26:69-75, emphasis added)

When Peter fell, it was at the worst possible time, and he fell hard—so hard that he must have thought there could be no recovery for him. That's why he wept so bitterly. Today we might say it was three strikes and Peter was out. Game over! His heart was broken.

If you or I had been betrayed by Peter like that, we might have been bitter. Would we have decided never to trust Peter again? Would we have pushed him away? Would we have decided never to speak to him again? Or if we had a message for him, what would it have been? It probably wouldn't have been positive. But after Jesus' resurrection, the angelic messenger made God's perspective clear when he met the women looking for Jesus at the tomb:

> But when they looked up, they saw that the stone, which was very large, had been rolled away. As they entered the tomb, they saw a young man dressed in a white robe sitting on the right side, and they were alarmed.
>
> "Don't be alarmed," he said. "You are looking for Jesus the Nazarene, who was crucified. He has risen! He is not here. See the place where they laid him. But go, *tell his disciples and Peter*, 'He is going ahead of you into Galilee. There you will see him, just as he told you.'" (Mark 16:4-7, emphasis added)

If the angel had said only, "Go tell his disciples," Peter and everyone else might have assumed that he wasn't to be included in the group anymore, that he was out. But the message was clear: God had not kept score, and the game was not over for Peter. He was still a disciple, and Jesus still had plans for him. That became crystal clear to Peter on a day he went fishing after the resurrection, and Jesus showed up on the shore to feed him, James, John, and four other disciples breakfast:

> When they had finished eating, Jesus said to Simon Peter, "Simon son of John, do you love me more than these?"

"Yes, Lord," he said, "you know that I love you."

Jesus said, "Feed my lambs."

Again Jesus said, "Simon son of John, do you love me?"

He answered, "Yes, Lord, you know that I love you."

Jesus said, "Take care of my sheep."

The third time he said to him, "Simon son of John, do you love me?"

Peter was hurt because Jesus asked him the third time, "Do you love me?" He said, "Lord, you know all things; you know that I love you." (John 21:15-17)

When Jesus asked Peter, "Do you love me?" the first time He used the word *agape*, which refers to divine unconditional love. Before his denial and failure, Peter probably would have boldly replied using *agape*, saying, "Of course I love you with that kind of unconditional love." But instead, knowing his own weakness, Peter responded that he loved Jesus using the word *phileo*, which is not divine unconditional love but rather a weaker human love. The second time Jesus asked, he used *agape* again. But the third time, Jesus changed the word in his question from *agape* to *phileo*. Jesus lowered his expectations to Peter's level. He wanted Peter to understand that he didn't expect him to give what he was incapable of. This gave Peter hope. It indicated that the love Peter was capable of giving, however imperfect or limited, would be enough for Jesus.

PUTTING COMPARISON TO REST

As much good as Jesus' reinstatement did for Peter, the disciple still needed one more lesson to help him finally put to rest the unhealthy habit of keeping score. After Peter said for the third time that he loved him, Jesus again told Peter to feed his sheep. And then he painted a picture of what Peter's reinstated life would look like in the future. But Peter couldn't resist comparing himself to others one more time:

> [Jesus said,] "Very truly I tell you, when you were younger you dressed yourself and went where you wanted; but when you are old you will stretch out your hands, and someone else will dress you and lead you where you do not want to go." Jesus said this to indicate the kind of death by which Peter would glorify God. Then he said to him, "Follow me!"
>
> Peter turned and saw that the disciple whom Jesus loved was following them. (This was the one who had leaned back against Jesus at the supper and had said, "Lord, who is going to betray you?") When Peter saw him, he asked, "Lord, what about him?"
>
> Jesus answered, "If I want him to remain alive until I return, what is that to you? You must follow me." Because of this, the rumor spread among the believers that this disciple would not die. But Jesus did

not say that he would not die; he only said, "If I want
him to remain alive until I return, what is that to you?"
This is the disciple who testifies to these things and
who wrote them down. We know that his testimony is
true. (John 21:18-24)

In response to Peter's attempt to compare himself to John, Jesus
made it clear that he would not allow it. In essence, he was
tearing up Peter's scorecard once and for all by telling him the
same thing he would say to us: instead of keeping score, just
follow me and do what I do.

TEAR UP YOUR SCORECARD

If Peter was able to come back from failure with Jesus' blessing
and fulfill his purpose, then we can too. And we can help and
encourage others to do the same—if we stop keeping score
ourselves.

Our desire as human beings is to keep score. I know that's
true of me. I'm naturally competitive. I want to win. But in my
early leadership years, a mentor gave me some advice. He said, "If
you're a leader, someone is going to hurt you. You have a choice.
You can carry that baggage today and tomorrow, or you can
let it go." I found what he said was true. Keeping score is like
carrying a suitcase around with you. The more you keep score,

the heavier it gets. And you take it everywhere you go. You drag
it to work with you. You take it to lunch with you. You sleep with
it. You feel the weight of it as you brush your teeth, exercise, or
spend time with your family. It's tiring.

It is better to tear up the scorecard, as God does. How can
you and I become more like Jesus and stop keeping score with
others? Start by doing three things:

1. Forgive Everyone, Because Everyone Needs Forgiveness

We all desperately desire forgiveness. As people who have
accepted Christ, we know the power of forgiveness. God is a
great forgiver and forgetter. Through the prophet Jeremiah,
God said, "I will forgive their wickedness and will remember
their sins no more" (31:34). God forgives the nightmares of our
past so we can reclaim our dreams of the future. To be like Jesus
and the Father, we must forgive.

> GOD FORGIVES THE NIGHTMARES OF OUR PAST SO WE CAN RECLAIM OUR DREAMS OF THE FUTURE.

We need to remember that
everyone else desperately desires
forgiveness as much as we do.
Even those who don't know Jesus
understand this desire. Novelist
Ernest Hemingway wrote a short
story called "The Capital of the
World" that opens this way:

Madrid is full of boys named Paco, which is the diminutive of the name Francisco, and there is a Madrid joke about a father who came to Madrid and inserted an advertisement in the personal columns of El Liberal which said: PACO MEET ME AT HOTEL MONTANA NOON TUESDAY ALL IS FORGIVEN PAPA and how a squadron of Guardia Civil had to be called out to disperse the eight hundred young men who answered the advertisement.[7]

I am Paco, and so are you. The world is filled with Pacos seeking to be forgiven.

To be like Jesus, we must share his desire to love others and forgive them because everyone needs to be forgiven. When Paul described *love* in his first letter to the Corinthians, he wrote, "Love is patient, love is kind. It does not envy, it does not boast, it is not proud. It does not dishonor others, it is not self-seeking, it is not easily angered, it keeps no record of wrongs" (1 Corinthians 13:4-5). Keeping no record of wrongs is simply another way of saying not to keep score.

Ephesians 4:32 says, "Be kind and compassionate to one another, forgiving each other, just as in Christ God forgave you." Forgiveness is not about keeping score; it is about losing count. And as Martin Luther King Jr. pointed out, "Forgiveness is not an occasional act; it is a permanent attitude. This was what Jesus

> "FORGIVENESS IS NOT AN OCCASIONAL ACT; IT IS A PERMANENT ATTITUDE. THIS WAS WHAT JESUS TAUGHT HIS DISCIPLES."
> —MARTIN LUTHER KING JR.

taught his disciples."[8] It is what Jesus is teaching us. And when you get weary of forgiving others, think of what Jesus told Peter, when he asked if forgiving someone seven times was enough: "Seven! Hardly. Try seventy times seven" (Matthew 18:22, MSG).

2. Stop Wanting to Be in First Place

Peter wasn't the only disciple who was ambitious and desired to be recognized as first in the class. James and his brother John had similar attitudes, as Mark recounts in his gospel:

> Then James and John, the sons of Zebedee, came to him. "Teacher," they said, "we want you to do for us whatever we ask."
>
> "What do you want me to do for you?" he asked.
>
> They replied, "Let one of us sit at your right and the other at your left in your glory."
>
> "You don't know what you are asking," Jesus said. "Can you drink the cup I drink or be baptized with the baptism I am baptized with?"

"We can," they answered. (Mark 10:35-40)

James and John were requesting the best seats in God's Kingdom. Why? Because they wanted to be first. And we know the rest of the apostles were no better than they were because later in the passage it says, "When the ten heard about this, they became indignant with James and John" (Mark 10:41). They wanted those seats too!

This became a great moment for Jesus to teach all of them about scorekeeping and why it's wrong:

> Jesus called them together and said, "You know that those who are regarded as rulers of the Gentiles lord it over them, and their high officials exercise authority over them. Not so with you. Instead, whoever wants to become great among you must be your servant, and whoever wants to be first must be slave of all. For even the Son of Man did not come to be served, but to serve, and to give his life as a ransom for many." (Mark 10:42-45)

Even though Jesus *was* first (Colossians 1:15-16), he didn't use his power to place himself first and make others feel inferior. Instead, he served people to show them how much he loved them. Look at another example of divine math, where Jesus' values feel opposite to the world's:

If I Want To...	I Must
Save my life	Lose my life
Be Lifted Up	Humble myself
Be the Greatest	Be a Servant
Be First	Be Last
Rule	Serve

Why does Jesus want us to live this way? Because *people* matter, not the score. You and I are bigger than the score to him! If we can stop wanting to be in first place, we will be more like Jesus.

3. Serve Others Instead of Expecting Others to Serve You

The best way to resist keeping score is to intentionally serve other people. Jesus modeled this in everything he did, but it was never more explicit than on the last night he spent with his disciples. Read this passage, which Chris shared in the previous chapter, this time presented in *The Message*:

> Jesus knew that the Father had put him in complete charge of everything, that he came from God and was on his way back to God. So he got up from the supper table, set aside his robe, and put on an apron. Then he poured water into a basin and began to wash the feet of the disciples, drying them with his apron. When he got

to Simon Peter, Peter said, "Master, *you* wash *my* feet?"

Jesus answered, "You don't understand now what I'm doing, but it will be clear enough to you later."

Peter persisted, "You're not going to wash my feet—ever!"

Jesus said, "If I don't wash you, you can't be part of what I'm doing."

"Master!" said Peter. "Not only my feet, then. Wash my hands! Wash my head!"

(John 13:3-9 , MSG)

Jesus was making the point that his leaders were not to keep score about status. Instead, they were to serve. Peter's reaction showed that he didn't yet understand. He wasn't opposed to having someone wash his feet. He just didn't want Jesus to do it, because Jesus was superior to him. But he thought of himself as superior to the rest of the disciples, so he likely would have been happy for one of *them* to wash his feet. And the other scorekeepers might have thought similarly. James might have thought, *I'm in the inner circle. Someone else ought to wash my feet.* John might have thought, *I'm Jesus' favorite. Someone else ought to wash my feet.* Andrew might have thought, *I'm the one who introduced Peter to Jesus. Someone else needs to wash my feet.*

It's notable the word *basin* is mentioned only twice in the Gospels. Both times the basin was used by a leader, and it revealed his character. Pilate, thinking of only himself, picked up a basin and used it to wash his hands of responsibility for what was about to happen to Jesus (Matthew 27:24). Jesus, thinking of others, picked up a basin and washed his disciples' feet.

If we want to be like Jesus, we need to become secure enough to serve others, letting Jesus keep score instead of us. There's a huge difference between secure and insecure followers of Christ:

The insecure are into titles—the secure are into towels.

The insecure are position-conscious—the secure are people-conscious.

The insecure want to receive value from others—the secure want to add value to others.

The insecure keep score—the secure don't keep score.

When we learn to serve others the way Jesus did, we become more confident in who we are and stop comparing ourselves to others. Instead of keeping score, we keep track—but of what we give because, like Jesus, we want to leave more than we take. Look at the difference between keeping score and keeping track:

Keeping Score	Keeping Track
Asks, "Am I getting a return from others?"	Asks, "Am I giving a return to others?"
Is Transactional	Is Transformational
Feeds on Competition	Feeds on Consideration
Waits to Be Served by Others	Readily Serves Others

To be like Jesus, we must adopt the attitude of Jesus, who said, "I've taken my place among you as one who serves" (Luke 22:27, MSG). We must become leaders who serve without keeping score.

At age seventy-seven, I still need to work to keep my competitive nature from rising in me and causing me to keep score with others. I continually coach myself in this area. Maybe you need to as well. When I turned sixty, I became especially aware of my drive to succeed and wanted God to help me replace it with a drive to serve. A few weeks before that milestone birthday, I wrote a prayer, which I still find myself needing to pray. It says,

> Lord, as I grow older, I would like to be known as . . .
> Available—Rather Than a Hard Worker
> Compassionate—More Than Competent
> Content—Not Driven
> Generous—Instead of Rich
> Gentle—Over Being Powerful
> A Listener—More Than a Great Communicator
> Loving—Versus Quick or Bright
> Reliable—Not Famous
> Sacrificial—Instead of Successful
> Self-controlled—Rather Than Exciting
> Thoughtful—More Than Gifted
> I Want to Be a Foot-Washer!

I believe there is hope for all of us to become foot-washers like Jesus. If you're ever in doubt, think about Peter. He went from denier of Jesus to proclaimer, from scorekeeper to soul-winner. On Pentecost, he preached the first gospel sermon delivered by anyone other than Jesus, and more than three thousand people came to Christ (Acts 2:14-41). Peter became one of the greatest Christian leaders in church history, and in the end, he did die for Jesus, as he once claimed he would.

Don't allow the negative actions of others to cause you to keep score. Don't let past hurts stop you from doing good. Don't fall into the condition described by Mark Batterson, who said, "We're paralyzed by things we *cannot change*—the past. We're crippled by things we *cannot control*—the future." Instead, follow his advice: "The solution? [William] Osler's age-old advice is as good a place to start as any: let go of 'dead yesterdays' and 'unborn to-morrows.'"[9]

> LET GO OF 'DEAD YESTERDAYS' AND 'UNBORN TO-MORROWS.'"
> —WILLIAM OSLER

Become a servant leader. Do what Jesus did—serve others without keeping score. If you do, you will discover that the observation of Rabbi Harold Kushner is true: "The purpose of life is not to win. The purpose of life is to grow and to share. When you come to look back on all that you have done in life, you will get more satisfaction from the pleasure you have brought into other people's lives than you will from the times that you outdid and defeated them."[10]

5

JESUS ACKNOWLEDGED HIS HUMANNESS

Chris Hodges

There is something endearing about a person who is authentic and real. They're not putting on a mask or pretending to be someone they're not. They're approachable because you know your experience with them reflects who they really are. You're drawn to them and want to learn from them, to follow their lead, and to be part of what they're all about.

High-road leaders embrace authenticity and sincerity. They're willing to be known for who they are, not for who others want them to be. They display self-awareness and reflect humility. And one of the greatest ways high-road leaders bring these qualities together in their leadership is by acknowledging their humanness.

FULLY MAN, FULLY GOD

Jesus modeled this value beautifully. Both fully God and fully man, Jesus was the incarnate Son of God, Immanuel, God with us in the flesh. He became human and dwelt among us so he could experience every aspect of humanity—the full range of what it means to live in a mortal body. He never hid his humanness. He let people see his grief as he wept over the loss of his dear friend Lazarus (John 11:33-35), his hunger (Matthew 21:18-19), and his longing for the support of his disciples the night before he died (Matthew 26:40-45).

Perhaps one of most powerful examples of Jesus displaying his humanness occurred as he hung on the cross. While experiencing excruciating pain, Jesus made seven statements that teach us how to take the high road while acknowledging our humanness:

- "Father, forgive them, for they know not what they do" (Luke 23:34, ESV) teaches us to forgive others no matter how brutal the offense.
- "Today you will be with me in paradise" (Luke 23:43) teaches us to help others who are experiencing our same struggles.
- "Woman, behold, your son!" and "Behold, your mother!" (John 19:26-27, ESV) teach us to take care of those closest to us.
- "My God, my God, why have you forsaken me?" (Matthew 27:46) teaches us to direct our hard questions to God.
- "I thirst!" (John 19:28, ESV) teaches us the importance of acknowledging our needs.

- "It is finished" (John 19:30) teaches us that in every struggle there is a purpose and an end.
- "Into your hands I commit my spirit" (Luke 23:46) teaches us to trust God.

The statement that stands out to me in the simple way it reveals the humanness of Jesus is "I thirst." It's so basic and so real. If the Son of God requested help during his bad day, we would be wise to remember that we, too, will have tough times when we need to ask for help, when we must acknowledge our humanness and allow others to help us.

WHY ARE WE RELUCTANT?

Many times we don't express our needs. It's human nature to conceal our feelings and humanness, often because we assume others will try to exploit our vulnerability rather than provide help. Leaders can be particularly reluctant to reveal their needs or ask for help. They assume others will view them as weak, undisciplined, or needy, believing, *If people really knew me, they wouldn't like me.* As a result, they fear intimacy and keep people from getting too close and seeing who they really are. They feel pressure to defend their image or protect their reputation as tough and determined. They fear letting others see their vulnerabilities, and they allow others to see only what they want them to see. They try to control their image and stick to a script, consequently coming across as guarded and inauthentic, even fake. And when we sense someone is being fake, they lose our trust.

If you've ever been burned in a relationship, whether personal or business, it's natural to protect yourself. You might take longer to trust someone or be more rigorous about doing your due diligence before partnering with them. As a result, you may keep others at arm's length to avoid experiencing another betrayal or rejection.

People also create distance when they know they've disappointed others. Perhaps no one understood the relationship between disappointment and distance better than Peter. As we've mentioned, even after Jesus told him, "This very night, before the rooster crows, you will disown me three times" (Matthew 26:34), even after Peter vowed, "Even if all fall away, I will not" (Mark 14:29), Peter denied knowing his Master—not once but, just as Jesus foretold, three times. Underlining his betrayal, Peter heard the rooster crow just as "the Lord turned and looked straight at Peter," and feeling the weight of his own disappointment, he "went outside and wept bitterly" (Luke 22:61-62).

Peter likely continued distancing himself after Jesus' death and resurrection by returning to what he knew best, what he had done prior to following Jesus for the previous three years— fishing. That is what Peter was doing when Jesus greeted him and some of the other disciples, pointing them to a massive catch and preparing breakfast for them on the beach (John 21:1-12).

Jesus acknowledged Peter's humanness by making it clear that He forgave Peter's past denials. The simple act of preparing a meal for Peter and the other disciples showed how attuned Jesus was to both their physical and emotional needs. When Peter recognized his risen Lord, the fisherman jumped into the water and rushed to shore. Knowing he was forgiven and pursued, Peter wanted to close the distance between them, literally as well as relationally.

Similar to Peter after denying Christ, we often attempt to hide our weaknesses by playing it safe and retreating to our comfort zone. If we can't avoid people, then we put up walls. When we do that, others tend to notice. They may view us as cordial but not comfortable, as wary but not warm. Others might even wonder if we're hiding something—which we are. We're hiding who we really are. We're convinced people wouldn't like us if they knew the real us, so we don't give them that opportunity. Rather than acknowledging our humanness in pursuit of intimacy, we consider it a weakness that must be hidden.

People often learn to wear masks and perform because of their desire for approval, and they continue this pattern for as long as it works. People who were not affirmed growing up may be

> WHEN WE ELEVATE THE OPINIONS OF OTHERS ABOVE WHAT GOD THINKS OF US, WE SET OURSELVES UP FOR FAILURE.

more susceptible to seeking praise and recognition, and they are concerned about what others think of them. But when we elevate the opinions of others above what God thinks of us, we set ourselves up for failure. As Proverbs says, "Fear of man will prove to be a snare, but whoever trusts in the LORD is kept safe" (29:25). Just as our hidden weaknesses make us distant, our desire for approval makes us defensive. In an effort to get someone to like us, we will often destroy other relationships.

STOP HIDING THE CRACKS

To be a high-road leader like Jesus, we must learn to drop our fear-based façade and stand in sincerity. In fact, the very origin of the word "sincerity" illustrates this point. In ancient times Greek artisans were known for making pottery that rarely cracked. Roman pottery, however, would often crack and need to be covered up and sealed with wax. Out of this practice came a familiar word highlighting the literal difference between the two kinds of pottery—the word *sincere*, meaning "without wax."

Sincere means not only genuine, but without covering up flaws and imperfections, without hiding cracks and rough edges. We see this referenced by the apostle Paul, who wrote, "We refuse to wear masks and play games. . . . Rather, we keep everything we do and say out in the open, the whole truth on display, so that those who want to can see" (2 Corinthians 4:2, MSG).

If we choose not to acknowledge our humanness and self-protectiveness takes root, we can become like the Grinch who stole Christmas in the classic Dr. Seuss story. Living in a cave, he bitterly plotted how to ruin their Christmas and spoil their joy. Even clearer, we see how this played out with a guy in the Bible named Job who lost everything. During a difficult season, his friends turned on him. "All my intimate friends detest me; those I love have turned against me" (Job 19:19).

As a result of all this, you might even become afraid of getting too close to God. Perhaps you feel let down by him or you've been burned by the church. Maybe your hurt has festered into distance that undermines your faith in God's goodness and your trust in his unconditional love for you. If that describes you, I want you to know that God wants to help you.

GOD WITH US

The truth is that Jesus understands exactly what you're going through. We're told that he was touched with the feeling of our infirmities (Hebrews 4:15). Jesus knows exactly what it feels like to be let down. He was betrayed by Judas, forgotten by Peter, misunderstood at the sham trial after his arrest. Others blasphemed and mocked him, ridiculing him for the truth he told. Jesus was stripped and humiliated, beaten and tortured, left to die like a common criminal. No wonder he felt forsaken on the cross and called out to God.

Through it all, Jesus modeled humanness and authenticity.

He went through every aspect of human life so we would be willing to approach him, knowing that he understands. We see this from the very beginning of his life on earth in perhaps my favorite part of the Christmas story:

> This is how Jesus the Messiah was born. His mother, Mary, was engaged to be married to Joseph. But before the marriage took place, while she was still a virgin, she became pregnant through the power of the Holy Spirit. Joseph, to whom she was engaged, was a righteous man and did not want to disgrace her publicly, so he decided to break the engagement quietly.
>
> As he considered this, an angel of the Lord appeared to him in a dream. "Joseph, son of David," the angel said, "do not be afraid to take Mary as your wife. For the child within her was conceived by the Holy Spirit. And she will have a son, and you are to name him Jesus, for he will save his people from their sins."
>
> All of this occurred to fulfill the Lord's message through his prophet:
>
> "Look! The virgin will conceive a child!
> She will give birth to a son,
> and they will call him Immanuel,
> which means 'God is with us.'"
> (Matthew 1:18-23, NLT)

Notice the importance of what this baby would be called. Matthew says, "They will call him Immanuel." Basically, Jesus had a nickname—Immanuel. Why would he be called that? Because it expressed an aspect of God that people had not experienced before—God in the flesh, right there with them. This contrasted dramatically with the religion the Jews had grown up learning.

> JESUS MODELED HUMANNESS AND AUTHENTICITY. HE WENT THROUGH EVERY ASPECT OF HUMAN LIFE SO WE WOULD BE WILLING TO APPROACH HIM, KNOWING THAT HE UNDERSTANDS.

Rather than distant in heaven, God was suddenly up close and personal. He was God with us!

God became a person. God dwelt among us. God was one of us. This theology of identification means that Jesus actually lived every part of life so he could identify with you and me. That's probably why he didn't start his public ministry until age thirty despite obviously being ready when he was twelve.

Jesus lived for thirty-three years on this earth so he could identify with us as humans. He is a personal God who understands exactly what it is like to have a heartbeat, to feel hunger pangs, to experience sore feet. He knew that identification would be vitally important. If you believe he understands you, then you will be willing to approach him:

For we do not have a high priest who is unable to
empathize with our weaknesses, but we have one who has
been tempted in *every way*, just as we are—yet he did
not sin. Let us then approach God's throne of grace
with confidence, so that we may receive mercy and find
grace to help us in our time of need."
(Hebrews 4:15-16, emphasis added)

And we *can* approach the throne of grace. Why? Because
he understands us in our time of need. There's no distance or
misunderstanding. Jesus knows because he has experienced it all.
The Message says it this way:

We don't have a priest who is out of touch with our
reality. He's been through weakness and testing,
experienced it all—all but the sin. So let's walk right up
to him and get what he is so ready to give. Take the
mercy, accept the help. (Hebrews 4:15-16, emphasis
added)

Jesus made himself vulnerable by becoming human and
experiencing everything you and I can ever face because he
knows the importance of identification and relatability.

   I've been ministering and preaching for more than forty years
now, and people respond more often to the stories I tell of my

failures and struggles than my victories and successes. When we show our weakness, it draws people to us. They relate to us and trust that we know who they are and how they struggle. It's why putting your ego aside is so important.

JESUS UNDERSTANDS US
AND OUR HUMANNESS

Consider the way someone who has had cancer immediately identifies with another cancer survivor. They have an immediate connection around the shared ordeal of receiving an unwanted diagnosis, choosing a treatment plan, suffering through that treatment, and experiencing life moving forward. Their bond is strong because they know they are understood and accepted by one another.

Similarly, Jesus understands because he has lived on earth in a human body made of flesh and blood. The One sitting on the throne, the God of the universe, our Creator, became a human being just like us and experienced everything you and I would experience, and so he totally understands. He gets us.

As a result of acknowledging his humanness, Jesus understands us in three distinct ways.

1. He Understands Relationships

After Jesus was born in Bethlehem, Mary and Joseph married and extended their family. Jesus had at least four brothers and two sisters, so he understood relationships. Once Jesus went public with his ministry, people began to talk about who he was and where he came from, saying, "Isn't this the carpenter? *Isn't this Mary's son* and the brother of James, Joseph, Judas and Simon? Aren't his sisters here with us?" (Mark 6:3, emphasis added).

Jesus knew what it was like to be teased by mean brothers. To feel protective about a sister. To experience sibling rivalry. To have a family who thought he was out of his mind: "When his family heard about this, they went to take charge of him, for they said, 'He is out of his mind'" (Mark 3:21). Most of us have at least one crazy person in our families, and if you think you don't, then that crazy person is probably you!

Seriously, though, has your family ever thought you were out of your mind? Been critical of a decision you were making? Questioned your actions in front of other people? Jesus knew what that was like. He knew what it's like to be accused, betrayed, rejected.

Jesus understood what it was like to be single. And he also understood what it is like to be married—to the church, the Bride of Christ. He knew what it was like for his spouse to cheat on him. He understood family problems and that human relationships can be especially painful.

2. He Understands Life

Our Savior also understands life because he lived on earth during a time when it wasn't particularly easy. He was born at a time when his homeland, Israel, had been conquered and annexed by the Roman Empire. His arrival was not in a royal palace with luxurious amenities but rather in a humble barn with a feed trough as a crib.

His life was tough. When he was barely a toddler, his family had to flee to Egypt for his safety. His earthly father was a tradesman, a carpenter, neither wealthy nor powerful. After beginning his public ministry, Jesus experienced skepticism and even ridicule. Many people scoffed at the idea that someone from "the other side of the tracks" could be the long-promised Messiah, the Son of God.

Hebrews says, "That's why he had to enter into *every detail of human life*. Then, when he came before God as high priest to get rid of the people's sins, he would have *already experienced it all himself*—all the pain, all the testing—and would be able to help where help was needed" (Hebrews 2:17-18, MSG, emphasis added). As our High Priest, Jesus knows the full extent of what it means to be human while also, in his holiness, being able to go before God the Father to expiate our sins.

So often we think of Jesus in a white robe, a preacher happily traipsing from place to place healing the sick, forgiving the sinners, and welcoming the outcasts. But such an inaccurate perspective misses so much of how Jesus acknowledged his humanness. Jesus fully understands the ups and downs of everyday life. We must remember that Jesus only spent three years ministering in public and leading the twelve disciples. Prior to that, he had spent roughly eighteen years doing manual labor as a carpenter, the trade he learned from Joseph.

Jesus' humble background may have caught some people by surprise even as it helped many others relate to him. I identify with that because I have always felt unqualified for what I do. I like to joke, "I'm basically just a C-student from Louisiana." But my comfort and candor about who I am and where I come from allows more people to connect with and trust me. They might not relate to someone who seems to have the perfect pedigree and offers all the right answers. Leaders endear themselves to others when they don't see themselves as self-qualified or world-qualified—but *God-qualified*. Paul described how this is often the way God chooses those he places in leadership:

> Brothers and sisters, think of what you were when you were called. Not many of you were wise by human standards; not many were influential; not many were of noble birth. But God chose the foolish things of the world to shame the wise; God chose the weak things of the world to shame the strong. God chose the lowly things of this world and the despised things—and the things that are not—to nullify the things that are, so that no one may boast before him. It is because of him that

you are in Christ Jesus, who has become for us wisdom from God—that is, our righteousness, holiness and redemption. Therefore, as it is written: "Let the one who boasts boast in the Lord." (1 Corinthians 1:26-31)

Jesus perfectly acknowledged his humanness as a high-road leader by upending expectations and working hard, with humility. Being a carpenter when Jesus lived didn't involve a trip to Lowe's or The Home Depot. There were no nail guns or power saws. Jesus measured and sawed, hammered and nailed, sanded and stained the old-fashioned way. If you've ever tried to work without power tools, then you know he had calloused hands and tender blisters. Undoubtedly, he understands what it is like to pay his bills. He understands what it's like when people try to cheat us. He understands what it is like when the economy is bad.

Throughout my life I've always been blessed with so much from God, but this hasn't prevented me from experiencing tough times. Perhaps the toughest time was when we first moved to Alabama more than twenty years ago to launch Church of the Highlands. Don't get me wrong—I loved every minute of it. But I remember paying bills over time instead of all at once and having to buy the medicine my son Joseph needed with credit cards. There were just so many unexpected expenses.

As I continued trusting God to provide, I found comfort and hope from realizing that Jesus knew exactly what it was like not

> JESUS UNDERSTANDS
> LIFE BECAUSE HE IS
> GOD WITH US.

to have a steady income or a healthy 401(k). He knows what it is like to live each day by faith, trusting the Father to provide. He understood then and he understands now—no matter what we're experiencing. Jesus understands life because he is God with us.

3. He Understands Pain

Finally, Jesus understands human pain. He experienced the emotional pain of rejection, abandonment, and mistreatment. About seven hundred years before Jesus walked the earth, the prophet Isaiah described Jesus' suffering: "He was *despised* and *rejected* by mankind, a man of *suffering*, and *familiar with pain*" (Isaiah 53:3, emphasis added).

Even before he went public with his ministry and revealed his identity as the Son of God, Jesus faced emotional pain. Surely he was ridiculed about his birth—in a stable, of all places. Then as now, a family had to be really poor for you to be born in a barn. From an earthly perspective, Jesus' birth was viewed as illegitimate since his mother was not married to her fiancé, Joseph. Consequently, Jesus was probably called the name associated with this kind of birth.

Jesus understands pain because he experienced it right up until his last dying breath. "If you are the Son of God," he heard others say, challenging his identity and mocking his powerlessness on the cross (Matthew 27:40). Rejected by the very people he helped and had come to save, Jesus suffered sadness and disappointment just as you and I have suffered.

Our Savior also understands physical pain as well. His physical ordeal leading to death on the cross had to be excruciating by all human standards. He experienced physical torture by three different groups who assaulted him—with a whip, nails, a crown of thorns, and a spear in his side. And yet he suffered his body's pain without complaining or whining, without raging or self-pitying. Jesus knew that his pain was not in vain:

> But he was pierced for our transgressions,
>   he was crushed for our iniquities;
> the punishment that brought us peace was on him,
>   and by his wounds we are healed. . . .
> He was oppressed and afflicted,
>   yet he did not open his mouth;
> he was led like a lamb to the slaughter,
>   and as a sheep before its shearers is silent,
>   so he did not open his mouth. (Isaiah 53:5, 7)

Jesus felt the pain of loss and the sting of grief. He knows what it's like to lose a loved one. He wept when his friend Lazarus died even though he knew that he would restore Lazarus and call him out of the tomb. But we also know of at least one other major loss in Jesus' life from implications of what he said from the cross.

There's only one reason why it would be necessary for Jesus to tell his mother, Mary, and his disciple John to take care of one another—Joseph must have died. Otherwise, Joseph would not only have been there, but would have been comforting his wife and sharing her grief at the suffering of Jesus. Feeling Joseph's absence and knowing his own death was imminent, Jesus wanted to make sure that his family took care of one another.

If you have ever lost someone close to you, then trust that Jesus understands. You can bring your pain before him and know that he completely understands because he has experienced the same pain. He's a God who is with you. There is nothing you have been through, are going through, or can go through that's beyond his experience.

As God incarnate in human form, Jesus revealed his humanity to make sure we can identify with him. He experienced the full range of human life so we can know that he fully understands us. Rather than remaining exalted in heaven, Jesus humbled himself in his humanness to become the ultimate servant leader, our Good Shepherd and Savior. He modeled the way of high-road leadership.

If Jesus was willing to acknowledge his humanness, why shouldn't you? As the apostle Paul stated, "All have sinned and fall short of the glory of God" (Romans 3:23). You're imperfect, and so am I. Let's own that and stop pretending otherwise. If we want to reach people for Jesus, we need to be vulnerable and open. We need to be like Jesus, the perfect example of humanness on the high road of leadership.

6

JESUS DID THE RIGHT THINGS FOR THE RIGHT REASONS

John C. Maxwell

Of all the teachings of Jesus, the Sermon on the Mount is his best known and most loved. In this lesson recorded by Matthew, Jesus communicated the values he wanted all his followers—then and now—to practice. At the heart of his message was the importance of doing the right things for the right reasons. He wanted his followers to do more than just obey the rules. He wanted our hearts to be sincere and our motives to be pure. Motives matter because people matter. Here is how Jesus began:

> Be especially careful when you are trying to be good so that you don't make a performance out of it. It might be good theater, but the God who made you won't be applauding.
>
> When you do something for someone else, don't call attention to yourself. You've seen them in action, I'm sure—"playactors" I call them—treating prayer meeting and street corner alike as a stage, acting compassionate

as long as someone is watching, playing to the crowds. They get applause, true, but that's all they get. When you help someone out, don't think about how it looks. Just do it—quietly and unobtrusively. That is the way your God, who conceived you in love, working behind the scenes, helps you out. (Matthew 6:1-4, MSG)

When I read Jesus' words, I feel a strong sense of conviction because Jesus is making it clear that our motives matter. I'm prompted to ask myself, *Why am I trying to be good? Is it for God or for others? Why am I trying to do good? Is it for myself or for others? Do I want the applause of people or the approval of God?* In everything we do, God knows why we do it. And he wants our motivation to align with his.

Why do we sometimes fail the motives test? Micah the prophet gave insight into the problem. He wrote,

[God's] already made it plain how to live, what to do, what God is looking for in men and women. It's quite simple: Do what is fair and just to your neighbor, be compassionate and loyal in your love, and don't take yourself too seriously—take God seriously. (Micah 6:8, MSG)

We often take ourselves too seriously and God not seriously enough. When we do that, it puts our focus on ourselves instead of on loving God and others, which is what God desires. Jesus addressed this specifically as he continued to deliver the Sermon on the Mount:

> And when you come before God, don't turn that into a theatrical production either. All these people making a regular show out of their prayers, hoping for fifteen minutes of fame! Do you think God sits in a box seat?
>
> Here's what I want you to do: Find a quiet, secluded place so you won't be tempted to role-play before God. Just be there as simply and honestly as you can manage. The focus will shift from you to God, and you will begin to sense his grace.
>
> The world is full of so-called prayer warriors who are prayer ignorant. They're full of formulas and programs and advice, peddling techniques for getting what you want from God. Don't fall for that nonsense. This is your Father you are dealing with, and he knows better than you what you need. (Matthew 6:5-8, MSG)

Our motives are wrong when we are number one on our agenda. Getting alone with God and being there as simply and honestly as we can shifts our focus to God, which is where it should be. With our focus on God, our motives become purified.

FINDING THE RIGHT REASONS

I am very aware that there is too much *me* in my motives, and I recognize that I need to get over myself. In fact, recently I got the chance to write a song about it with Bobby Hamrick, Chris August, and James Slater in Nashville called "Get Over Myself." I love the chorus:

> I've got to find myself
> To know myself
> To be myself
> To improve myself
> To get over myself
> So I can give myself to you.

I've studied leadership for more than fifty years, and for many decades, the organizations I founded have trained and developed leaders around the world. There's one characteristic we discovered is present in all leaders, regardless of their country, culture, gender, or level of experience: Leaders always see *more* than others see, and they see *before* others see. I call this ability in leaders to see more and before the "leadership advantage." They have a perspective that others don't have. It gives them a head start in seizing opportunities, solving problems, and pursuing advantages in the marketplace. If you possess the leadership advantage, you are faced with a choice. Will you use it to benefit yourself or others?

Low-Road Leaders use it to help only themselves.

Middle-Road Leaders use it to help themselves first before helping others.

High-Road Leaders use the leadership advantage to help others.

What you do depends on your motives. When you lead others for their benefit or for mutual advantage, you're motivating them. When you lead others only for your own benefit, you're manipulating. Since it's easy to cross the line from motivation to manipulation, let me show you the difference:

Motivation	Manipulation
Is for Your Advantage	Is for My Advantage
Cares about Results and the Person	Cares Only about Results
Is Fueled by Love	Is Fueled by Pride
Empowers People	Controls People
Values People	Devalues People
Fosters Loyalty	Fosters Resentment
Takes the High Road	Takes the Low Road

Jesus was always on the side of motivation and never manipulated anyone. We should follow his example.

> WHAT YOU DO DEPENDS ON YOUR MOTIVES.... WHEN YOU LEAD OTHERS ONLY FOR YOUR OWN BENEFIT, YOU'RE MANIPULATING.

Recently I developed a friendship with Don Wenner. He is the Founder and CEO of DLP Capital, which has been on the list of fastest growing private companies in America for the last eleven years and possesses more than $5 billion in assets under their management.[11] Don is a very successful businessperson, but his focus is primarily on investing in, developing, and financing affordable housing for people who need it. Why? Because when he was a child, Don's family had very little money and continually moved from place to place trying to find good affordable housing. Growing up, Don moved thirty-seven times! His childhood difficulty motivated him to build affordable communities so that other children would live a better life. He says he tries to live by a verse he often quotes: "To whom much is given, much will be required" (see Luke 12:48).[12] He is using his leadership advantage to serve others.

LOVE IS ALWAYS THE *RIGHT REASON*

Jesus never failed to see God's bigger picture and act for the right reasons. He always valued relationships over rules, truth over law, and servanthood over religion. He never allowed legalism to displace love. Over and over you see him responding to people with love:

- When Peter walked on the water and began to sink, Jesus lifted him up, taking the high road when another failed (Matthew 14:31).
- Upon hearing of John the Baptist's death, Jesus withdrew to be alone. However, when the multitude followed him, he didn't become impatient. He felt compassion and healed the sick (Matthew 14:13-14).
- Jesus washed the feet of Judas even though he knew the disciple would betray him. He never allowed someone else's actions to determine his (John 13:5).
- Jesus healed the servant of the high priest who came to arrest him after Peter cut off his ear, demonstrating how to love an enemy and setting new standards of behavior (John 18:10-11).
- When challenged by the high priest, Jesus remained silent, knowing he was headed to the cross to save us (Matthew 26:62-63).

> JESUS ALWAYS VALUED RELATIONSHIPS OVER RULES, TRUTH OVER LAW, AND SERVANTHOOD OVER RELIGION. HE NEVER ALLOWED LEGALISM TO DISPLACE LOVE.

One of the easiest places to see Jesus' motivation is in the way he approached the Sabbath. For example, when Jesus and his disciples were walking through a grainfield on the Sabbath, here's what happened:

One Sabbath day he was walking through a field of ripe grain. As his disciples made a path, they pulled off heads of grain. The Pharisees told on them to Jesus: "Look, your disciples are breaking Sabbath rules!"

Jesus said, "Really? Haven't you ever read what David did when he was hungry, along with those who were with him? How he entered the sanctuary and ate fresh bread off the altar, with the Chief Priest Abiathar right there watching—holy bread that no one but priests were allowed to eat—and handed it out to his companions?" Then Jesus said, "The Sabbath was made to serve us; we weren't made to serve the Sabbath." (Mark 2:23-27, MSG)

The Gospels record Jesus helping and healing broken people on the Sabbath, proof that he loved people, not the man-made rules of the religious leaders.

> Then he went back in the meeting place where he found a man with a crippled hand. The Pharisees had their eyes on Jesus to see if he would heal him, hoping to catch him in a Sabbath violation. He said to the man with the crippled hand, "Stand here where we can see you."
>
> Then he spoke to the people: "What kind of action suits the Sabbath best? Doing good or doing evil? Helping people or leaving them helpless?" No one said a word.
>
> He looked them in the eye, one after another, angry now, furious at their hard-nosed religion. He said to the man, "Hold out your hand." He held it out—it was as good as new! The Pharisees got out as fast as they could, sputtering about how they would join forces with Herod's followers and ruin him. (Mark 3:1-6, MSG)

When you love people, value them, and want to help them, it's very difficult for your motives to be wrong.

WHEN GOOD INTENTIONS GO WRONG

Jesus was often tested by people who put rules over relationships. Those leaders were guilty of what we would today call *legalism*, and Jesus was especially hard on them. They pretended to be perfect, and instead of loving others, they demanded that others follow rules they couldn't follow themselves. Jesus said, "They crush people with unbearable religious demands and never lift a finger to ease the burden." And then later, "What sorrow awaits you teachers of religious law and you Pharisees. Hypocrites! For you are so careful to clean the outside of the cup and the dish, but inside you are filthy—full of greed and self-indulgence" (Matthew 23:4, 25, NLT).

Legalism not only condemns people when Jesus didn't; it also promotes dogmatism. How? We tend to turn our personal experiences into convictions which we impose on others without Jesus' blessing. For example, suppose I sense the Lord wants me to eat an orange. In obedience, I eat the orange because that is what I sincerely believe God has led me to do. The next day, I sense that I should eat an orange again. So far so good.

> LEGALISM NOT ONLY CONDEMNS PEOPLE WHEN JESUS DIDN'T; IT ALSO PROMOTES DOGMATISM.

But what often happens? On the third or fourth day, I decide to create a rule for myself to eat an orange every day. At this point, I'm no longer looking to and listening for the Holy Spirit to guide me. Instead, I rely on a law.

Inventing laws creates barriers in my relationship with God because I practice a rule instead of pursuing my relationship with him. That stunts my spiritual growth. It kills life because what I did in the Spirit yesterday, I do in the flesh today. And when my pious effort to follow my law succeeds, my ego becomes gratified, which leads to self-righteousness. What's even more damaging is when I start applying my rules to others. If I insist that *my* conscience become *your* guide, my motives are wrong and I'm traveling the low road, not the high road of selflessness.

How can you and I guard against legalism? We know we're off the high road when we are . . .

- Pretending that we can measure up to God by keeping rules that we have written.
- Trying to create morality from the outside in rather than the inside out.
- Focusing on cultural conformity instead of Biblical spirituality.
- Judging others because they don't fit our rules.

> IF I INSIST THAT *MY* CONSCIENCE BECOME *YOUR* GUIDE, MY MOTIVES ARE WRONG AND I'M TRAVELING THE LOW ROAD, NOT THE HIGH ROAD OF SELFLESSNESS.

One of the most striking examples of someone doing the right things for the wrong reasons can be found in the story Jesus told of the Prodigal Son. The younger son, who asked for his share of the inheritance and blew it all on wild living, did the wrong things for the wrong reasons. But when he repented, humbled himself, and returned home, he was accepted by his father with love and forgiveness. And his father was so excited about his return that he threw a party. The person with the problem was the older brother. He was doing the right things, but with the wrong motives. Here's what Jesus said about him:

All this time his older son was out in the field. When the day's work was done he came in. As he approached the house, he heard the music and dancing. Calling over one of the houseboys, he asked what was going on. He told him, "Your brother came home. Your father has ordered a feast—barbecued beef!—because he has him home safe and sound."

The older brother stomped off in an angry sulk and

refused to join in. His father came out and tried to talk to him, but he wouldn't listen. The son said, "Look how many years I've stayed here serving you, never giving you one moment of grief, but have you ever thrown a party for me and my friends? Then this son of yours who has thrown away your money on whores shows up and you go all out with a feast!"

His father said, "Son, you don't understand. You're with me all the time, and everything that is mine is yours—but this is a wonderful time, and we had to celebrate. This brother of yours was dead, and he's alive! He was lost, and he's found!" (Luke 15:25-32, MSG)

The older brother stayed on the farm, did the chores, and saw his father every day, but he didn't have the heart of the father. Every day the older son was doing the right things, but without the right motives. Every day his actions were right, but his attitude was wrong. Every day he was close to his father, but he didn't connect with him. He didn't long to see his lost brother return. And he didn't share the joy of his father when his brother did come home. Maybe the older son thought he had to earn his place; he certainly didn't understand that everything his father had was already his.

We must guard ourselves against becoming like the older brother. Our motives matter to God. Jesus communicated God's perspective on this when quoted the prophet Hosea, saying, "I desire mercy, not sacrifice" (Matthew 9:13). God wants us to love people. The apostle Paul reinforced this truth in his first letter to the Corinthians. He said we can do great things—speak in tongues, deliver prophecies, exhibit mountain-moving faith, fathom mysteries, possess knowledge, give to the poor, and endure hardship—but if we "do not have love," we "gain nothing" (1 Corinthians 13:1-3).

FORGIVENESS IS ALWAYS THE *RIGHT THING*

One of the greatest expressions of love is forgiveness. It is the ultimate right thing for the right reason. It is the heart of the gospel message because Jesus came and died on the cross to forgive you, me, and everyone else who repents. I know the power of forgiveness because I have been the recipient of Jesus' grace. But I have also seen the power of forgiveness among people who don't yet follow Christ. My non-profit organization, the Maxwell Leadership Foundation, is working in many countries teaching values to people in an effort to transform their nations. Of all the values people learn in transformation roundtables, *forgiveness* has the greatest impact. We hear stories of relationships reconciled, lives saved, and families transformed by its power.

High-road living means forgiving others. Jesus emphasized the importance of forgiveness when he included it in his teaching on prayer. After praising God, we can ask him to do many things for us: grant us provision, give

> ONE OF THE GREATEST EXPRESSIONS OF LOVE IS FORGIVENESS. IT IS THE ULTIMATE RIGHT THING FOR THE RIGHT REASON.

us protection, and deliver us from evil. But Jesus also includes one thing we must do: forgive others. He said, "Forgive us our debts, *as we also have forgiven* our debtors" (Matthew 6:12, emphasis added). And in case there was a chance his listeners missed the point, Jesus added a commentary to make it clear. He said, "For if you forgive other people when they sin against you, your heavenly Father will also forgive you. But if you do not forgive others their sins, your Father will not forgive your sins" (Matthew 6:14-15).

Followers of Christ who are high-road leaders understand that forgiveness is a big deal to God. Author and pastor Bruce Wilkinson explained both the value and the difficulty of forgiving others:

> Forgiveness is one of the most unnatural responses in all of human nature. Think about it. Selfless giving is hard enough, but forgiving? That's like lavishing the

best gift ever on the person who just robbed you!

Why should a mother forgive the drunk driver who killed her son? . . . Or a teenager forgive the father who left when she was a baby and has never made an effort to see her since? Or a businessman forgive the partner who asked for his all, then betrayed his trust? At those times everything in us cries out for justice, retribution, fairness—not forgiveness.[13]

Yet that is what Jesus asks us to do. He set the standard. And we will be judged by that standard. Do you freely forgive others? Do you really want God to use the way you do or don't forgive other people as the barometer for how he will forgive you? I don't. That helps me remember to do the right thing for the right reasons. I work to forgive, even when I find it hard to do. As former chaplain of the US Senate Lloyd John Ogilvie said, "The hardest time to be gentle is when we know we are right and someone else is obviously dead wrong." But he also points out, "We hold the power to give or refuse a blessing" when someone has failed us.[14]

> "THE HARDEST TIME TO BE GENTLE IS WHEN WE KNOW WE ARE RIGHT AND SOMEONE ELSE IS OBVIOUSLY DEAD WRONG."—LLOYD JOHN OGILVIE

Forgiveness is a powerful force. It not only blesses others, but it also changes our hearts. That's no small task, and it's something rules cannot accomplish. Many people would rather rewrite a law because it's easier than rewriting a heart. But when our hearts change, we become more like Jesus. Only a changed heart will do the right things for the right reasons.

TAKING HIGH-ROAD INITIATIVE

One of the most powerful things you can do as a follower of Christ is keep doing the right things for the right reasons even when people criticize, blame, or try to harm you. Nobody did this better than Jesus. Many years ago, Kent M. Keith wrote a piece he called "Paradoxical Commandments of Leadership" describing the difficult actions of people and how we should respond to them.[15] I want to share Keith's words along with the ways Jesus took the high road with people in the face of opposition:

People are illogical, unreasonable, and self-centered. Love them anyway. As Jesus was being crucified, he said, "Father, forgive them, for they do not know what they are doing" (Luke 23:34).

If you do good, people will accuse you of selfish ulterior motives. Do good anyway. After Jesus performed miracles of healing, his critics said, "He is possessed by Beelzebul! By the prince of demons he is driving out demons" (Mark 3:22), but Jesus continued to heal the sick and drive out demons.

If you are successful, you win false friends and true enemies. Succeed anyway. The crowds who cheered Jesus on Sunday, saying, "Blessed is the king who comes in the name of the Lord! (Luke 19:38), cried out on Friday, "Crucify him!" (John 19:15). And Jesus gave his life for them.

The good you do today will be forgotten tomorrow. Do good anyway. After healing a group of lepers, Jesus asked, "Were not all ten cleansed? Where are the other nine? Has no one returned to give praise to God except this foreigner?" Then he said to the one who returned, "Rise and go; your faith has made you well" (Luke 17:17-19).

Honesty and frankness make you vulnerable. Be honest and frank anyway. Confiding in his disciples, Jesus said, "Do you think I came to bring peace on earth? No, I tell you, but division" (Luke 12:51).

JESUS DID THE RIGHT THINGS FOR THE RIGHT REASONS 121

The biggest men with the biggest ideas can be shot down by the smallest men with the smallest minds. Think big anyway. During the Last Supper, as Jesus told his disciples he would be betrayed, "A dispute also arose among them as to which of them was considered to be greatest" (Luke 22:24). Jesus told them, "The greatest among you should be like the youngest, and the one who rules like the one who serves" (Luke 22:26).

People favor underdogs, but follow only top dogs. Fight for a few underdogs anyway. When people brought children to Jesus to be blessed, his disciples tried to shoo them away. But Jesus said, "Let little children come to me, and do not hinder them, for the kingdom of God belongs to such as these" (Mark 10:14).

What you spend years building may be destroyed overnight. Build anyway. In the Garden of Gethsemane, Judas came forward and kissed Jesus. "Then men stepped forward, seized Jesus and arrested him. . . . All the disciples deserted him and fled" (Matthew 26:50, 56).

People really need help but may attack you if you do help them. Help people anyway. After Jesus started his ministry, he went to the synagogue in his hometown to let them know he wanted to help them by reading from Isaiah: "The Spirit of the Lord is on me, because he has anointed me to proclaim good news to the poor. He has sent me to proclaim freedom for the prisoners and recovery of sight for the blind, to set the oppressed free, to proclaim the year of the Lord's favor" (Luke 4:18-19). Their response was to drive him out of town (Luke 4:29).

Give the world the best you have and you'll get kicked in the teeth. Give the world the best you have anyway. Jesus stood innocently before the crowd that wanted to kill him. "'Which of the two do you want me to release to you?' asked the governor. 'Barabbas,' they answered. 'What shall I do, then, with Jesus who is called the Messiah?' Pilate asked. They all answered, 'Crucify him!'" (Matthew 27:21-22).

If Jesus, in the face of such opposition and hatred, could love and trust people anyway, do good anyway, serve people anyway, build anyway, help people anyway, and give his best anyway, we can make the effort to do the right things for the right reasons every day. That is the best way to show Jesus that we love him and be salt and light in a world that feels like it's getting darker.

7

JESUS EMBRACED AUTHENTICITY
Chris Hodges

Jesus knew who he was. There was no pretense with Jesus, no pomp and circumstance. No robes or special place where he stood under the spotlight. No special privileges or reserved parking places that designated his authority and position. He never would have waited in the green room to be escorted onto a stage ten minutes after worship started to avoid the crowds. Jesus cut through all the church stuff and anything inauthentic. Jesus modeled how high-road leaders should act based on knowing who they are. He was authentic through and through.

Authenticity matters because it garners respect and invites others to be authentic as well. Even if the people you lead do not agree with you, they will respect you if you are authentic. They will see that you are the same person at work as you are in line at Starbucks or at home with your family. High-road leaders practice authenticity by doing what they say they will do and aligning their actions with their words.

Without authenticity, there will be a glaring gap between what you *say* you believe and what you are *actually doing*. Others will notice and realize you hold them to one standard and make yourself the exception. Jesus challenged the leadership of his time by calling out this kind of hypocrisy: "The teachers of the law and the Pharisees sit in Moses' seat. So you must be careful to do everything they tell you. But do not do what they do, for they do not practice what they preach" (Matthew 23:2-3).

In contrast, Jesus always practiced what he preached. His authenticity as both God and man revealed his Father's love in action: "The Word [God] became a human being and lived here with us. We saw his true glory, the glory of the only Son of the Father. From him the complete gifts of underserved grace and truth have come down to us" (John 1:14, CEV). Jesus was the ultimate real-deal, authentic high-road leader, humbling himself so that he would exalt his heavenly Father and serve those around him. To be more like him, we need to be willing to be our authentic selves.

I AM, THEREFORE I DO

Jesus was comfortable with who he was because he knew his true identity. If you desire to lead people, you must be aware of and accept your authentic self before you can allow others to know who you are and communicate to them why they should follow you. Throughout the Gospel of John, Jesus defined himself to others using what I call his *I am* declarations. These four statements show us what to do to embrace authenticity as high-road leaders like Jesus:

1. Jesus Said: "I Am the Bread of Life."

Therefore, I Say: "I Will Nourish Others through My Contribution."

Jesus offered everyone true fulfillment. He said, "I am the bread of life. Whoever comes to me will never go hungry, and whoever believes in me will never be thirsty" (John 6:35). He made this statement because he knew what he had to offer—that who he was would satisfy and nourish every soul. He was prompted to make this statement shortly after feeding the five thousand by blessing one boy's lunch of five loaves and two fish, using what was available to provide sustenance to the hungry crowd (John 6:1-13). Why? Because the crowd was asking for more bread or manna such as God provided to the Israelites as they trekked to the Promised Land. Jesus was making it clear he is the source; he is the bread of life.

High-road leaders embrace authenticity because they know what they have to offer to others. In every setting in which we find ourselves, we

> JESUS SAID: "I AM THE BREAD OF LIFE." THEREFORE, I SAY: "I WILL NOURISH OTHERS THROUGH MY CONTRIBUTION."

should ask, *What do I have to give that would satisfy a longing, a need of those around me?* rather than *What can this do for me?* We need to focus on our contribution for others' benefit, as Jesus did.

2. Jesus Said: "I Am the Light of the World."

Therefore, I Say: "I Will Turn on the Light and Make Things Brighter."

When Jesus said, "I am the light of the world. Whoever follows me will never walk in darkness, but will have the light of life" (John 8:12), he made it clear that he illuminates darkness and brings light and life to those who follow him. Jesus offers real forgiveness with authentic love and grace rather than shame and condemnation.

So many times we feel insecure and worry about how God views our mistakes. For that reason, when Jesus says, "I am the light of the world," many of us assume he came to put a bright glaring light on our faults and failures. But that's not what Jesus does. He brings life to us by shining his light on our dark places. As John states, "For God did not send his Son into the world to condemn the world,

> JESUS SAID: "I AM THE LIGHT OF THE WORLD." THEREFORE, I SAY: "I WILL TURN ON THE LIGHT AND MAKE THINGS BRIGHTER."

but to save the world through him" (John 3:17). God loves you just as you are—but he loves you too much to leave you that way. And he wants you to share his love with others, to be a light in the darkness.

3. Jesus Said: "I Am the Gate."

Therefore, I Say: "I Will Open Doors and Show Others the Way."

Jesus stated, "I am the gate; whoever enters through me will be saved. They will come in and go out, and find pasture" (John 10:9). He was describing a new way of relating to God that people could experience. Drawing on the relationship between sheep and the caring shepherd who tends them, Jesus emphasized the importance of trust. We can recognize the loving power of Jesus and rest in the security of his protection. Jesus also said, "My sheep listen to my voice; I know them, and they follow me. I give them eternal life, and they shall never perish; no one will snatch them out of my hand" (John 10:27-28).

Just as the Good Shepherd set boundaries for his sheep, so we must set them for the people we lead. We must provide access and also protection. A good

> JESUS SAID: "I AM THE GATE." THEREFORE, I SAY: "I WILL OPEN DOORS AND SHOW OTHERS THE WAY."

shepherd—a high-road leader following the example of Jesus—will lay down his life for his sheep. Authentic relationships occur when others realize you are willing to die to yourself in order to lead and serve them, to show them the way and open doors to help them.

4.   Jesus Said: "I Am the Resurrection."

Therefore, I Say: "I Will Bring New Life to Every Encounter with Others."

Finally, Jesus said, "I am the resurrection and the life. The one who believes in me will live, even though they die; and whoever lives by believing in me will never die. Do you believe this?" (John 11:25-26). The real future he offers goes beyond mortal limits. What Jesus gives is an eternal promise, not a temporary fix. He anchors us in our identity as a beloved child of God, fearfully and wonderfully made. He empowers us to discover and live out our divine purpose. He guides us as our Good Shepherd who knows what we need better than we do.

> JESUS SAID: "I AM THE RESURRECTION." THEREFORE, I SAY: "I WILL BRING NEW LIFE TO EVERY ENCOUNTER WITH OTHERS."

To be high-road leaders like Jesus, we should constantly be looking for ways to bring new life to those around us. How can we infuse every relationship with resurrection power? One way is simply by giving others another chance when they've missed the mark. The world is so quick to write people off—one and done. But like Jesus, we should look for ways to bring every dead end back to life and give others a fresh start. Jesus set the example for us that not even *death* is final. It's never too late to experience a rebirth, a renewal, a resurrection.

PLANKS BEFORE SPECKS

Jesus valued authenticity. He lived, taught, and stood up for it and challenged people to respond to the conviction of authenticity. He had little regard for religious institutional hypocrisy or individuals who were hypocrites. He specifically challenged his followers to focus on their own shortcomings rather than looking to blame or condemn others:

> Why do you look at the speck of sawdust in your brother's eye and pay no attention to the plank in your own eye? How can you say to your brother, "Let me take the speck out of your eye," when all the time there is a plank in your own eye? You hypocrite, first take the plank out of your own eye, and then you will see clearly to remove the speck from your brother's eye. (Matthew 7:3-5)

To lead others effectively, we must focus on the plank in our own eye before calling out the speck of sawdust in someone else's. We must model an awareness of our weaknesses, flaws, and mistakes and possess a willingness to seek forgiveness. High-road leaders do not pretend that they have everything together or that they have arrived at perfection. They are real with people.

The contrast between authenticity and hypocrisy was highlighted during the encounters Jesus had with the Jewish religious leaders. They often laid plans to trap him or bait him to take political positions. In one of those encounters,

> The Pharisees went out and laid plans to trap him in his words. They sent their disciples to him along with the Herodians. "Teacher," they said, "we know that you are a man of integrity and that you teach the way of God in accordance with the truth. You aren't swayed by others, because you pay no attention to who they are. Tell us then, what is your opinion? Is it right to pay the imperial tax to Caesar or not?"
>
> But Jesus, knowing their evil intent, said, "You hypocrites, why are you trying to trap me? Show me the coin used for paying the tax." They brought him a denarius, and he asked them, "Whose image is this? And whose inscription?"
>
> "Caesar's," they replied.
>
> Then he said to them, "So give back to Caesar what is Caesar's, and to God what is God's."

When they heard this, they were amazed. So they
left him and went away. (Matthew 22:15-22)

Jesus always saw clearly through these traps and exposed the
religious leaders' hypocrisy. He called out the Pharisees even
more directly in another instance, telling his disciples and the
crowd that had gathered, "They tie up heavy, cumbersome loads
and put them on other people's shoulders, but they themselves
are not willing to lift a finger to move them" (Matthew 23:4).
Jesus consistently humbled himself, always setting the example
through his incarnation as God with us of how to lead by serving
with authenticity.

Contrast Jesus' actions with those of the Jewish religious
leaders who continually tried to hide their own insecurities and
shame by focusing on external appearances rather than internal
integrity. Jesus pointed out:

> Everything they do is done for people to see: They make
> their phylacteries wide and the tassels on their garments
> long; they love the place of honor at banquets and the
> most important seats in the synagogues; they love to be
> greeted with respect in the market-places and to be called
> "Rabbi" by others. (Matthew 23:5-7)

In other words, they only cared about the title, the status,
the perception—and not the responsibility, the privilege,
the substance—of leading authentically. They worked hard

to appear righteous, holy, and devoted to God, but their hypocrisy betrayed their sinful, self-centered hearts, which Jesus consistently exposed and rebuked. Seven times in Matthew 23:13-32, Jesus said, "Woe to you, teachers of the law and Pharisees," calling them hypocrites and describing them as cups washed on the outside but not the inside. Rather than authentic, they were full of pretense, pushing people to appear a certain way even if they didn't correct what was inside.

Not only did Jesus call out the pretense and hypocrisy of the Pharisees, but he also made clear the importance of sincerity, honesty, and humility.

> To some who were confident of their own righteousness and looked down on everyone else, Jesus told this parable: "Two men went up to the temple to pray, one a Pharisee and the other a tax collector. The Pharisee stood by himself and prayed: 'God, I thank you that I am not like other people—robbers, evildoers, adulterers—or even like this tax collector. I fast twice a week and give a tenth of all I get.'
>
> "But the tax collector stood at a distance. He would not even look up to heaven, but beat his breast and said, 'God, have mercy on me, a sinner.'
>
> "I tell you that this man, rather than the other, went home justified before God. For all those who exalt themselves will be humbled, and those who humble themselves will be exalted." (Luke 18:9-14)

Jesus showed how authenticity and hypocrisy are polar opposites. When we avoid the vulnerability of authenticity and choose the safety and self-righteousness of hypocrisy, we create barriers to our relationships with ourselves, others, and God. Hypocrisy hinders us from seeing ourselves because we're hiding parts of ourselves due to shame, insecurity, or inadequacy. We don't want to face the truth, let alone allow others to see it. When we do this, it creates a domino effect, preventing others from knowing the gift of who we really are, flaws and all. Hiding behind hypocrisy also hinders our ability to accept and experience God's grace. When we can't see God accurately, then others cannot see him authentically and accurately through us.

> WHEN WE AVOID THE VULNERABILITY OF AUTHENTICITY AND CHOOSE THE SAFETY AND SELF-RIGHTEOUSNESS OF HYPOCRISY, WE CREATE BARRIERS TO OUR RELATIONSHIPS WITH OURSELVES, OTHERS, AND GOD.

GETTING REAL

Jesus modeled the value of authenticity by being open and transparent about his own struggles. On the night before his death, a short time before Judas betrayed him, Jesus went to the garden of Gethsemane to pray:

> He took Peter and the two sons of Zebedee along with him, and he began to be sorrowful and troubled. Then he said to them, "My soul is overwhelmed with sorrow to the point of death. Stay here and keep watch with me." (Matthew 26:37-38)

Jesus acknowledged that he wanted to be with his disciples and to pray. He didn't pretend to be tough or stoic, indifferent to the suffering he was facing. Instead, he expressed his authentic emotions and asked those closest to him to be with him and keep watch. Jesus needed them so much that he even stopped praying to go to them, but he found them sleeping! If Jesus was willing to embrace authenticity in that way, then we should be willing to risk vulnerability as well.

Sadly, many of us have been conditioned by culture and rewarded socially for doing the exact opposite—hiding our true feelings and covering up our vulnerable needs. We view vulnerability as a weakness rather than a strength. I remember a lady who called our church once wanting to know if we offered counseling. As she talked to someone from our staff, she revealed that she was already a believer and belonged to a solid biblical church. She knew she needed counseling to deal with her personal struggles but couldn't bring herself to share with those in her own Christian community.

High-road leaders who follow the example of Christ don't hide their struggles or pretend to have all the answers. We can experience the freedom to be authentic because we know that our weakness is made perfect in his strength. We can risk being known. We no longer need to indulge in harmful deception born out of our fears and insecurities. As Paul said, "We refuse to wear masks and play games. We don't maneuver and manipulate behind the scenes.... Rather, we keep everything we do and say out in the open" (2 Corinthians 4:2, MSG).

> WE KNOW THAT OUR WEAKNESS IS MADE PERFECT IN HIS STRENGTH. WE CAN RISK BEING KNOWN.

God never intended for us to do life alone, and deep down we know this. We long to be free of posturing and posing, trying to please others or project a certain image. We want to be known for who we are—including the emotions and struggles that make us fearful and insecure—and accepted and loved by those around us. The wisdom of Ecclesiastes reinforces the benefit of being connected to others in a way that comes only with authenticity:

Two are better than one,
      because they have a good return for their labor:
If either of them falls down,
      one can help the other up.

But pity anyone who falls
    and has no one to help them up.
Also, if two lie down together, they will keep warm.
    But how can one keep warm alone?
Though one may be overpowered,
    two can defend themselves.
A cord of three strands is not quickly broken.
(Ecclesiastes 4:9-12)

Everybody wants meaningful relationships, to be seen for who we are and to experience the freedom to be authentic. Remember the theme song for the old sitcom *Cheers*? It's a reminder of how desperately we long to take a break from all the worries and cares we face in the world and to find a sense of belonging, comfort, and welcome in a place "where everybody knows your name." I think you will agree that the best place for this should be the church—not the bar!

Real life change happens in the context of relationships where we are free to be our messy, glorious selves. Where we know that we are wanted, and in turn we want to do life with those in community with us. As Paul said about us in the body in Christ, "So we belong to each other, and each needs all the others." (Romans 12:5, TLB). Jesus chose his disciples not because they were perfect or would do everything right. He chose them to free them to be who God created them to be. And he did that by embracing authenticity.

OPENING A WINDOW
TO AUTHENTICITY

Why are authentic relationships so important? Simply put, they help us know ourselves better, know others better, and know God better. But that doesn't mean they come naturally. No, we have to cultivate them.

One tool that I've found helpful in thinking through the value of authentic relationships is called the Johari Window. Developed by psychologists Joseph Luft and Harrington Ingham in 1955, this tool helps us understand ourselves, which in turn makes us more authentic. The Johari Window reveals four areas of awareness. Here's my take on each of the four areas:

	Known to Self	Unknown to Self
Known to Others	Arena	Blind Spot
Unknown to Others	Mask	Potential

Arena

This first quadrant reflects the public "you," representing what you and others know about you. If we prioritize this aspect of ourselves above all others, we resort to superficial living, trying to appear bigger on the outside than we are on the inside. As we've mentioned, Jesus confronted the religious leaders of his day for working so hard to appear religious: "Everything they do is done *for people to see*: They make their phylacteries wide and the tassels on their garments long" (Matthew 23:5, emphasis added). To be a high-road leader like Jesus, you must seek God's approval above other people's and allow the arena to reflect an alignment of both your external and internal selves.

Mask

This pane of the window represents what we know about ourselves but hide from others—our secrets and hidden thoughts and emotions. We all have areas we want to hide, but we cannot be authentic if we're hiding. People stay as sick as their secrets. To be like Jesus, we must be transparent and vulnerable. Even though we know we should, we still struggle at times. We continue to wear masks to hide those dark areas of our lives and experiences.

The devil knows this is where real life change takes place. So he attacks our relationships aggressively, using the ways we put ourselves above others to cause harm, misperception, and pain. The enemy would much rather we defend and protect ourselves by hiding behind masks than risk authenticity that connects hearts, forgives offenses, and heals wounds.

This is where we need to do most of the work to become authentic. Rather than giving in to our fear and apprehension about revealing our true selves or being hurt, we must let others in on our struggles, our burdens, and our wounds. Rather than isolating ourselves and hiding behind masks, we need to show our hearts and discover authentic connection. Professor, novelist, and apologist C. S. Lewis said, "Friendship is born at that moment when one person says to another, 'What! You too? I thought I was the only one.'"[16] When we are honest and authentic, we inspire others to let down their masks and be known as well.

Within the context of authentic relationships, we can tell the truth about our fears and problems, share our secrets and shame, and enjoy accountability because we have someone watching over our soul who is reminding us of what is true about who we are and what we are called to do.

To sustain authentic relationships and experience the full benefits of being known and knowing others, we must confess and pray. God's Word is clear: "Confess your sins to each other and pray for each other so that you may be healed" (James 5:16). We can tell our secrets, ask for forgiveness, and accept the fullness of God's grace extended through other people.

> "FRIENDSHIP IS BORN AT THAT MOMENT WHEN ONE PERSON SAYS TO ANOTHER, 'WHAT! YOU TOO? I THOUGHT I WAS THE ONLY ONE.'"
> – C. S. LEWIS

And we should pray for others without ceasing, maintaining our loving concern and connection, similar to the actions of a believer named Epaphras described in Colossians. Paul said he was "always wrestling in prayer" for others to help them "stand firm in all the will of God, mature and fully assured" (Colossians 4:12).

Blind Spot

The third quadrant indicates things others can see about you, but you can't. We need to do the work to know what we don't know if we hope to be authentic. Early on, my wife and I worked out signals for when we have something caught in our teeth, or, even worse, something dangling from our nose. No one wants the distraction and embarrassment of such moments, so we need help from others who are willing to have our backs and show us what we do not know or realize about ourselves.

While Jesus had no blind spots, he showed his awareness of this quadrant when he asked his disciples who people said he was (Matthew 16:13). After they reported that some said he must be John the Baptist or Elijah, perhaps Jeremiah or another prophet,

Jesus asked them who *they* said he was. Peter declared that he was the Messiah, the Son of the living God (verse 16). However, shortly after this declaration, Peter insisted that Jesus must not submit to the betrayal and death awaiting him. In response, Jesus rebuked Peter, comparing such an idea to a temptation from the enemy (verse 23). Jesus was pointing out Peter's blind spot.

For you to develop authenticity in this quadrant, you must be in relationships with people you trust. You need faithful friends who know you and care for you who are willing to point out your blind spots—not acquaintances, critics, or enemies. Proverbs says, "Faithful *are* the wounds of a friend, but the kisses of an enemy *are* deceitful" (27:6, NKJV).

Real friends are honest with you. They don't always tell you what you want to hear. They have your back and lift you up when you stumble. They see through your masks and love the real you, the authentic you. And they prevent you from succumbing to discouragement. They follow the advice given in Hebrews: "See to it, brothers and sisters, that none of you has a sinful, unbelieving heart that turns away from the living God. But encourage one another daily, as long as it is called 'Today,' so that none of you may be hardened by sin's deceitfulness" (Hebrews 3:12-13).

Everyone needs friends like that. And every follower of Christ who takes the high road *becomes* a friend like that.

Potential

The fourth quadrant represents what you and others don't know about yourself. These are the things that only God knows. You have unrealized potential, and you will never reach it alone. You need others to help you discover it, exercise it, and refine it. "As iron sharpens iron, so one person sharpens another" (Proverbs 27:17).

In a community of people committed to authenticity, you discover that *we* is more powerful than *me*. Collaboration and cooperation with others produce results that are more than the sum of individual contributions. Authentic people in community provide support and encouragement, constructive feedback and suggested strategies for improvement, knowing that this is how everyone grows and fulfills their potential. We need each other because "the whole body, supported and held together by its ligaments and sinews, grows as God causes it to grow" (Colossians 2:19). So instead of just being you, be part of *we*. Being part of others' lives at a heart level produces a greater awareness of the impact that authenticity can have, helping us to know others and be known, to enjoy the fulfillment of our God-given potential as leaders.

Embracing authenticity as Jesus modeled it requires us to acknowledge our strengths and our weaknesses, our reliance on God and our need for other people. When you commit to being authentic, you inherently invest in your integrity. Jesus wants you to commit to being the same person whether you're in front of a group or the last in line, whether you're enjoying the fruits of success or struggling to maintain growth. High-road leaders know that embracing authenticity draws them closer to Jesus even as it points others to him as well. Embrace authenticity the way Jesus did, and you'll be astounded by the change in your life and your impact on others.

IN A COMMUNITY OF PEOPLE COMMITTED TO AUTHENTICITY, YOU DISCOVER THAT *WE* IS MORE POWERFUL THAN *ME*. COLLABORATION AND COOPERATION WITH OTHERS PRODUCE RESULTS THAT ARE MORE THAN THE SUM OF INDIVIDUAL CONTRIBUTIONS.

8

JESUS PLACED PEOPLE ABOVE HIS AGENDA

John C. Maxwell

What does it mean to be a leader? What does it mean to be a *Christian* leader? It means serving others. Jesus said, "Anyone who wants to be first must be the very last, and the servant of all" (Mark 9:35). That means continually placing people above your own agenda. That's what Jesus did as he walked the earth and interacted with people.

We too easily forget this as leaders. We tend to want to elevate ourselves. We somehow think leadership should put us above others, even though Jesus didn't model that. Chuck Colson, a lawyer who worked for President Nixon in the White House, was jailed for his involvement in Watergate. He later became a follower of Christ, wrote about the misconceptions people have about leadership, and pointed out how Jesus was a different kind of leader. He recalled a conversation he had with the president:

> One brisk December night as I accompanied the president from the Oval Office in the West Wing of

the White House to the Residence, Mr. Nixon was musing about what people wanted in their leaders. He slowed a moment, looking into the distance across the South Lawn, and said, "The people really want a leader a little bigger than themselves, don't they, Chuck?" I agreed. "I mean someone like de Gaulle," he continued. "There's a certain aloofness, a power that's exuded by great men that people feel and want to follow."

Jesus Christ exhibited none of this self-conscious aloofness. He served others first; He spoke to those to whom no one spoke; He dined with the lowest members of society; He touched the untouchables. He had no throne, no crown, no bevy of servants or armored guards. A borrowed manger and a borrowed tomb framed His earthly life.

Kings and presidents and prime ministers surround themselves with minions who rush ahead, swing the doors wide, and stand at attention as they wait for the great to pass. Jesus said that He Himself stands at the door and knocks, patiently waiting to enter our lives.[17]

> JESUS WALKED LOVINGLY WITH LOWLY PEOPLE TO SHOW US HOW TO LIVE ON THE HIGH ROAD.

Jesus, the king of kings, did not make himself a king, president, or prime minister on this earth. He walked lovingly with lowly people to show us how to live on the high road.

JESUS REACHED OUT TO PEOPLE OTHERS DISMISSED

During the time Jesus was on earth, women and children had no social standing and were often overlooked and dismissed. But not by Jesus. He placed them above his agenda and made it clear to others they were valuable and should be valued by them. Remember what happened when mothers brought their children to Jesus to receive a blessing? Every Jewish mother of that time wanted their children to be blessed by a Rabbi, especially around the time of their first birthday. Jesus understood this.

> People were bringing little children to Jesus for him to place his hands on them, but the disciples rebuked them. When Jesus saw this, he was indignant. He said to them, "Let the little children come to me, and do not hinder them, for the kingdom of God belongs to such as these. Truly I tell you, anyone who will not receive the kingdom of God like a little child will never enter it." And he took the children in his arms, placed his hands on them and blessed them. (Mark 10:13-16)

By blessing children, Jesus showed how much he valued both the children and their mothers, for he placed both above his agenda.

There are many examples in the Gospels of Jesus showing women love and respect while others devalued them. He showed them kindness, forgave their sins, and welcomed them to travel with him and his disciples. In other words, he placed them at the top of his agenda while others put them at the bottom of theirs. For example, consider this incident is recorded in Luke:

> When one of the Pharisees invited Jesus to have dinner with him, he went to the Pharisee's house and reclined at the table. A woman in that town who lived a sinful life learned that Jesus was eating at the Pharisee's house, so she came there with an alabaster jar of perfume. As she stood behind him at his feet weeping, she began to wet his feet with her tears. Then she wiped them with her hair, kissed them and poured perfume on them.
>
> When the Pharisee who had invited him saw this, he said to himself, "If this man were a prophet, he would know who is touching him and what kind of woman she is—that she is a sinner."
>
> Jesus answered him, "Simon, I have something to tell you."
>
> "Tell me, teacher," he said.
>
> "Two people owed money to a certain moneylender. One owed him five hundred denarii, and the other fifty. Neither of them had the money to pay him back,

so he forgave the debts of both. Now which of them will love him more?"

Simon replied, "I suppose the one who had the bigger debt forgiven."

You have judged correctly," Jesus said.

Then he turned toward the woman and said to Simon, "Do you see this woman? I came into your house. You did not give me any water for my feet, but she wet my feet with her tears and wiped them with her hair. You did not give me a kiss, but this woman, from the time I entered, has not stopped kissing my feet. You did not put oil on my head, but she has poured perfume on my feet. Therefore, I tell you, her many sins have been forgiven—as her great love has shown. But whoever has been forgiven little loves little."

Then Jesus said to her, "Your sins are forgiven."

The other guests began to say among themselves, "Who is this who even forgives sins?"

Jesus said to the woman, "Your faith has saved you; go in peace." (Luke 7:36-50)

Religious people like Simon the Pharisee wanted nothing to do with anyone like this woman. They saw her as a second-class citizen because she was a woman, and her sinful life made her an outcast. But she knew Jesus would value her, like he did all lost people, which is why she went to him and was so grateful for his acceptance and forgiveness. And Jesus' behavior attracted other women to him and became a catalyst for their wanting to travel with Jesus and his disciples to support them. Luke 8:1-3 says,

> After this, Jesus traveled about from one town and village to another, proclaiming the good news of the kingdom of God. The Twelve were with him, and also some women who had been cured of evil spirits and diseases: Mary (called Magdalene) from whom seven demons had come out; Joanna the wife of Chuza, the manager of Herod's household; Susanna; and many others. These women were helping to support them out of their own means.

Jesus valued and forgave a woman caught in adultery when the religious leaders tried to use her to trap him (John 8:1-11). He went out of his way to save an immoral Samaritan woman who was despised by her community (John 4:1-42). He healed a woman subject to bleeding and blessed her, saying, "Daughter, your faith has healed you. Go in peace and be freed from your suffering" (Mark 5:34).

People of all kinds sought out Jesus because they felt valued and respected by him. And he always gave them hope, not only by his actions, but with his words. Jesus said:

- "Who needs a doctor: the healthy or the sick? Go figure out what this Scripture means: 'I'm after mercy, not religion.' I'm here to invite outsiders" (Matthew 9:12-13, MSG).
- "I am the bread of life. Whoever comes to me will never go hungry" (John 6:35).
- "Anyone who drinks the water I give will never thirst—not ever" (John 4:14, MSG).
- "I came so they can have real and eternal life, more and better life than they ever dreamed of" (John 10:10, MSG).
- "I, when I am lifted up from the earth, will draw all people to myself" (John 12:32).

When we value people, give them hope, and place them above our agenda, we become like Jesus.

CONTINUAL INTERRUPTIONS

Look at the life of Jesus recorded in the Gospels, and you see that most of Jesus' ministry consisted of interruptions. When he had a choice between ignoring the needs of someone so that he could continue with his original plan or pausing and placing someone else's needs ahead of his agenda, Jesus chose

> IF WE OPEN OUR EYES AND SEE THE WORLD THE WAY JESUS DID, WE'LL RECOGNIZE THAT MUCH OF THE MINISTRY WE CAN DO IN THIS LIFE WILL CONSIST OF OPPORTUNITIES DRESSED UP AS INTERRUPTIONS.

the latter. If we open our eyes and see the world the way Jesus did, we'll recognize that much of the ministry we can do in this life will consist of opportunities dressed up as interruptions.

Look at the many ways Jesus was interrupted and turned these interruptions from potential irritations into ministry opportunities by placing people above his agenda. I've emphasized each of the interruptions with italics:

Jesus Performed a Miracle Instead of Enjoying a Party with His Friends

Jesus' earliest recorded miracle occurred before he started his formal ministry. He and his disciples were guests at a wedding banquet when his mother, Mary, asked for help.

> When they started running low on wine at the wedding banquet, Jesus' mother told him, "They are just about out of wine."

Jesus said, "Is that any of our business, Mother— yours or mine? *This isn't my time. Don't push me.*" (John 2:3-4, MSG)

But Jesus put people ahead of his agenda and saved the day. He asked the servants to fill large jars with water, which he turned into wine, and when the host tasted it, he declared, "You've saved the best till now!" (John 2:10, MSG).

Jesus Healed the Sick When He Wanted to Get Away for Much-Needed Solitude

When he learned his cousin John the Baptist had been executed by Herod Antipas, Jesus felt the need to get away from people. But people were always pursuing him.

> As soon as Jesus heard the news, he left in a boat to a remote area to be alone. But the crowds heard where he was headed and followed on foot from many towns. *Jesus saw the huge crowd as he stepped from the boat, and he had compassion on them and healed their sick.*
> (Matthew 14:13-14, NLT)

Even after serving the people in that way, Jesus still thought more about them than himself. His disciples wanted him to send the crowd away, but Jesus said, "That isn't necessary" (verse 16, NLT), and he went on to feed five thousand of them.

Jesus Stopped Eating Dinner to Defend a Woman Who Anointed Him

As the chief priests and elders plotted Jesus' death, he and his disciples were eating dinner together when a woman anointed Jesus:

> When Jesus was at Bethany, a guest of Simon the Leper, a woman came up to him as he was eating dinner and anointed him with a bottle of very expensive perfume. When the disciples saw what was happening, they were furious. "That's criminal! This could have been sold for a lot and the money handed out to the poor."
>
> *When Jesus realized what was going on, he intervened.* "Why are you giving this woman a hard time? She has just done something wonderfully significant for me." (Matthew 26:6-10, MSG)

He went on to tell his followers she would always be remembered and admired for what she had done (verse 13).

Jesus Stopped to Heal Two Blind Men Instead of Leaving Jericho

Jesus often moved from place to place teaching his followers. As he was preparing to travel toward Jerusalem, he was willing to delay his agenda to help people who shouted for his help. The

Gospel of Matthew states:

> As Jesus and the disciples left the town of Jericho, a large crowd followed behind. Two blind men were sitting beside the road. When they heard that Jesus was coming that way, they began shouting, "Lord, Son of David, have mercy on us!"
>
> "Be quiet!" the crowd yelled at them.
>
> But they only shouted louder, "Lord, Son of David, have mercy on us!"
>
> *When Jesus heard them, he stopped and called, "What do you want me to do for you?"*
>
> "Lord," they said, "we want to see!" *Jesus felt sorry for them and touched their eyes.* Instantly they could see! Then they followed him. (Matthew 20:29-34, NLT)

Jesus didn't allow the negative shouts of the crowd to dissuade him from placing these men above his agenda.

Jesus Paused His Teaching to Heal a Paralyzed Man

One of the most dramatic "interruptions" in Jesus' ministry occurred while he was teaching in a house filled with people. Mark says,

> After a few days, Jesus returned to Capernaum, and word got around that he was back home. A crowd

gathered, jamming the entrance so no one could get in or out. He was teaching the Word. They brought a paraplegic to him, carried by four men. When they weren't able to get in because of the crowd, they removed part of the roof and lowered the paraplegic on his stretcher. *Impressed by their bold belief, Jesus said to the paraplegic, "Son, I forgive your sins."* (Mark 2:1-5, MSG)

Teaching the Word of God was important to Jesus, yet he stopped speaking to forgive the man's sins and to heal his paralysis (Mark 2:8-12).

Jesus Visited the Home of a Tax Collector Instead of Passing Him By

The road from Galilee to Jerusalem went through the city of Jericho. Luke 19 says that Jesus was *passing through* the city when his journey was interrupted by an opportunity to place someone above his agenda:

Jesus entered Jericho and was passing through. A man was there by the name of Zacchaeus; he was a chief tax collector and was wealthy. He wanted to see who Jesus was, but because he was short he could not see over the crowd. So he ran ahead and climbed a sycamore-fig tree to see him, since Jesus was coming that way.

When Jesus reached the spot, he looked up and said

to him, "Zacchaeus, come down immediately. I must stay at your house today." So he came down at once and welcomed him gladly.

All the people saw this and began to mutter, "He has gone to be the guest of a sinner."

But Zacchaeus stood up and said to the Lord, "Look, Lord! Here and now I give half of my possessions to the poor, and if I have cheated anybody out of anything, I will pay back four times the amount."

Jesus said to him, "Today salvation has come to this house, because this man, too, is a son of Abraham. For the Son of Man came to seek and to save the lost." (Luke 19:1-10)

Jesus suspended his journey because Zacchaeus was eager to meet him, and Jesus wanted to spend time with a man who was financially wealthy but spiritually bankrupt. He didn't care that others would criticize him. High-road leaders would rather do the right thing and be talked about poorly than do the wrong thing and be praised. He wanted to see salvation come to Zacchaeus, and he did.

While it's true that Jesus prioritized self-care and often retreated to quiet places to pray, whenever he was around people, he put them first. Time after time in the Gospels when Jesus was busy, he stopped what he was doing and placed people ahead of his agenda. People who follow in Jesus' footsteps understand that God wants us to do the same. Theologian Henri J. Nouwen wrote,

> A few years ago I met an old professor at the University of Notre Dame. Looking back on his long life of teaching, he said with a funny twinkle in his eyes: "I have always been complaining that my work was constantly interrupted, until I slowly discovered that my interruptions were my work."
>
> That is the great conversion in life: to recognize and believe that the many unexpected events are not just disturbing interruptions of our projects, but the way in which God molds our hearts and prepares us for his return.[18]

WHEN GOD ASKS US TO STOP WHAT WE ARE DOING, HE IS OFTEN GIVING US A CHANCE TO BE A PART OF WHAT *HE IS DOING*.

When God asks us to stop what we are doing, he is often giving us a chance to be a part of what *he is doing*. In God's Kingdom, an interruption often becomes an invitation to doing something better.

THE ESSENCE OF PUTTING OTHERS FIRST

When Jesus came to earth and started modeling high-road leadership, he challenged everyone to rethink how they interacted with others, and he called them to a higher level of living. In the Sermon on the Mount, Jesus said,

> You're familiar with the old written law, "Love your friend," and its unwritten companion, "Hate your enemy." I'm challenging that. I'm telling you to love your enemies. Let them bring out the best in you, not the worst. When someone gives you a hard time, respond with the supple moves of prayer, for then you are working out of your true selves, your God-created selves. This is what God does. He gives his best—the sun to warm and the rain to nourish—to everyone, regardless: the good and bad, the nice and nasty. If all you do is love the lovable, do you expect a bonus? Anybody can do that. If you simply say hello to those who greet you, do you expect a medal? Any run-of-the-mill sinner does that.
>
> In a word, what I'm saying is, *Grow up*. You're kingdom subjects. Now live like it. Live out your God-created identity. Live generously and graciously toward others, the way God lives toward you.
>
> (Matthew 5:43-48, MSG)

High-road leadership requires us to treat others better than they treat us. That's what we're doing when we place people ahead of our agenda. We're serving people following Jesus' example. We're giving others our best because we're grateful God has given us his best. And that helps us to grow up into the kind of people Jesus wants us to be.

SERVANTHOOD WILL SURPRISE YOU

In 1987, I read Eugene Habecker's book *The Other Side of Leadership*. In it, he quoted John White:

> The true leader serves. Serves people. Serves their best interests, and in so doing will not always be popular, may not always impress. But because true leaders are motivated by loving concern rather than a desire for personal glory, they are willing to pay the price.[19]

Habecker's book, and especially that quote, made a strong impression on me. It was my first informal introduction to the idea of becoming a high-road leader. Reading the book, I felt challenged to become the kind of leader Jesus was.

That kindled my desire to place people above my own agenda, which at times I found to be difficult. I was a leader accustomed to pursuing a vision at full speed. I had to slow down, listen to people, stop what I was doing, and serve others. At first, I did it out of a sense of duty because I knew it was what Jesus wanted. But in time, it began to change me. And some of those changes surprised me. What I expected from serving others and what resulted were very different:

What I Thought: Serving Others Is What I Should Do

What I Got: A Heart That Valued People— Surprise!

When I first started placing people above my agenda and serving them, I felt I was above them, reaching down to give them assistance. That's when I discovered that my attitude was wrong. Here's what I learned:

> SERVING BECAUSE YOU SEE PEOPLE AS VALUABLE SHIFTS YOU FROM FEELING LIKE YOU ARE ABOVE THEM TO PUTTING YOUR-SELF BELOW THEM TO LIFT THEM UP.

If we see others as weak, we will try to help them.
If we see others as broken, we will try to fix them.
But if we see others as valuable, we will serve them.

Serving because you see people as valuable shifts you from feeling like you are above them to putting yourself below them to lift them up. Changing my attitude changed my heart. Knowing God values someone and serving them for that reason makes serving them a joy.

What I Thought: Serving Others Is Seldom Noticed

What I Got: I Was Noticed, and Serving People Became My Identity—Surprise!

Frederick L. Collins said, "Always remember there are two types of people in the world: those who come into a room and say, 'Here I am!' and those that come in and say, 'Ah, there you are!'"[20] Focusing on others and serving them is a way of saying, "There you are." It lets them know they're important. Do that enough, and it becomes part of you. One doesn't expect any fanfare for that. However, keep serving others and your actions will be noticed because the desire to serve is so rare in this world.

> "THERE ARE TWO TYPES OF PEOPLE IN THE WORLD: THOSE WHO COME INTO A ROOM AND SAY, 'HERE I AM!' AND THOSE THAT COME IN AND SAY, 'AH, THERE YOU ARE!'"—FREDERICK L. COLLINS

What I Thought: Serving Others Is a Private Action

What I Got: Serving Others Is a Contagious Action—Surprise!

Only once did Jesus spell out that he was giving his disciples an example for them to follow. That was when he washed their feet. But that private experience of servanthood became a public experience. Jesus asked his followers to serve others in the same way. When people do that and discover the joy of seeing others valued and loved, they want to give that experience to others. Serving becomes contagious.

What I Thought: Serving Others Is Important to People

What I Got: Serving Others Is Important to Jesus—Surprise!

Jesus made it clear in Matthew that the way we treat others is very important to him. Describing his future judgment of the sheep (those who follow him) and the goats (those who don't), Jesus said he will invite his sheep to enjoy their eternal reward:

> Take what's coming to you in this kingdom. It's been ready for you since the world's foundation. And here's why:

I was hungry and you fed me,
I was thirsty and you gave me a drink,
I was homeless and you gave me a room,
I was shivering and you gave me clothes,
I was sick and you stopped to visit,
I was in prison and you came to me.

Then those "sheep" are going to say, "Master, what are you talking about? When did we ever see you hungry and feed you, thirsty and give you a drink? And when did we ever see you sick or in prison and come to you?" Then the King will say, "I'm telling the solemn truth: Whenever you did one of these things to someone overlooked or ignored, that was me—you did it to me." (Matthew 25:35-40, MSG)

JESUS CARES SO MUCH ABOUT HOW WE TREAT OTHERS THAT HE TAKES IT PERSONALLY.

Jesus cares so much about how we treat others that he takes it personally. When you put people first and serve them, you're pleasing Jesus in ways you may not even be aware of. And Jesus will reward you for it in eternity.

How can we get close to Jesus and show him how much we love him? By serving others. Every time we place others ahead of our agenda, we are serving Jesus. What a privilege! There may be no greater way to please Jesus than by placing people above our own agenda. There may be no action we can take that makes us more like Jesus than placing people above our own agenda. It was what Jesus always did. We should strive to follow his example.

9

JESUS BROUGHT PEOPLE TOGETHER

Chris Hodges

During his time on earth, Jesus brought people together in ways that continue to change the world. He never compromised truth to draw people together, and everything he did was fueled by grace. While Jesus knew that some people would reject him and his radical message, that some would reject him and persecute his followers, he always sought to unite people with his Father and one another. Like every high-road leader, Jesus understood that bringing people together results in a powerful unity that is greater than the sum of its individuals.

Looking at the twelve people chosen by Jesus as his closest disciples, we see a diverse group of personalities. There were down-to-earth, working-class fishermen such as Peter, Andrew, James, and John (Matthew 4:18–22). There was Matthew, a tax collector (Mark 2:14), an unpopular profession known for its corruption. And there was Simon the Zealot (Matthew 10:4), a political revolutionary devoted to overthrowing the Romans and restoring Israel. This was not a group of men who would hang out together if not for the One they all followed.

In fact, if you gave them personality tests or skill-set assessments, you probably wouldn't choose them to work together. But Jesus poured his life into them, and they became unified as disciples and followers of Christ—and they changed the world. Jesus is the ultimate high-road leader because he saw beyond the external differences and internal variations of the people he brought together, seeing that it would allow them to sharpen one another and to fulfill their potential. Jesus knew bringing people together frees them to be who God created them to be. We should invite people to come together for the same purpose.

> JESUS KNEW BRINGING PEOPLE TOGETHER FREES THEM TO BE WHO GOD CREATED THEM TO BE.

WORD MADE FLESH

Sadly, we live in a world today that seems to encourage and celebrate division. People are pressured to choose a side and focus on the differences between themselves and others—cultures, backgrounds, skin colors, religious beliefs, political positions, and worldviews—rather than connecting based on what they have in common. Too often, division relies on drawing a line between your side and the other side, between what you believe versus what others believe.

Anytime people polarize into fractured factions, they lose more than they gain. The same happens when we emphasize truth over grace. People will respond to the gospel invitation when they know they are respected and accepted. They will welcome the truth if they experience kindness. Too frequently, people are hammered with truth rather than massaged with grace. Based on the example of Jesus, we are called to show God's love to others through our actions. Our message is truth, and our behavior is love. We can teach truth, but to bring people together the way Jesus did, we must be filled with love.

> OUR MESSAGE IS TRUTH, AND OUR BEHAVIOR IS LOVE. WE CAN TEACH TRUTH, BUT TO BRING PEOPLE TO-GETHER THE WAY JESUS DID, WE MUST BE FILLED WITH LOVE.

Truth and grace should never be separated. Why?

- We cannot overlook God's *truth* or grace loses its power.
- We cannot overlook God's *grace* or truth loses its penetration.
- Without truth, we are limited by our humanity and can only be nice to people.
- Without grace, we are limited by God's holiness and can only judge ourselves and others.

Truth without grace becomes mean-spirited, leverage for being right rather than for bringing people together in relationship. You won't win others to Jesus with arguments, evidence, and debate even if you're right because God has called us to be loving, like his Son. As Mother Teresa said, "If you judge people, you have no time to love them."[21]

> GRACE INVITES US TO BE FREE SO THE TRUTH CAN SET US FREE. GRACE PROVIDES THE GLUE THAT BRINGS PEOPLE TOGETHER.

Similarly, grace without truth becomes impotent. If we just accept everyone and everything as is, we deny the need for transformation. And there's no power to change. Grace invites us to be free so the truth can set us free. Grace provides the glue that brings people together.

Jesus literally embodied both truth and grace, and he related to everyone he encountered without compromising either. He fulfilled the truth of the law through his sacrifice for our sins, offering us salvation as a gift, something we cannot earn. Anyone can receive it simply by asking for it and allowing God's Spirit into their lives. The essence of grace is unmerited favor. Instead of receiving the punishment we deserve for our sins, Jesus paid our debt. Jesus exceeded all expectations; he turned the other cheek, went beyond all extra miles, and laid down his life for us.

AS I HAVE LOVED YOU

In order to bring people together as Jesus did, we must remember that our goal is not to be right but to be in relationship. We are called to love as he loved. For us to have relationships with others, they must see and experience God's love through us—not just in what we say but by what we do. Jesus said, "A new command I give you: Love one another. As I have loved you, so you must love one another. By this everyone will know that you are my disciples, if you love one another" (John 13:34-35).

How will everyone know we are followers of Jesus? We might be tempted to fill in the blank with "church attendance" or "Bible knowledge," with "faithful giving" or "exemplary behavior." But that's not what Jesus said. No, he said that everyone will know you are my disciples if you *love one another*. How you treat people—how well you love them—reveals what you believe and have experienced in your own life. When you love people as Jesus loved, you accept them without approving of their sin.

If we want to be high-road leaders who bring people together, we need to realize that we cannot *antagonize* and *appeal* at the same time. This explains why the Bible says, "The *only thing that counts* is faith expressing itself through *love*" (Galatians 5:6, emphasis added).

How can we express our faith through love? By the way we serve people. Accepting people as genuine friends and helping them in practical ways shows we care about them—not just an agenda. When we practice being a good listener, we let others know our love is real. When we consciously focus our concern on meeting their needs, we demonstrate the compassion of Christ.

> IF WE WANT TO BE HIGH-ROAD LEADERS WHO BRING PEOPLE TOGETHER, WE NEED TO REALIZE THAT WE CANNOT *ANTAGONIZE* AND *APPEAL* AT THE SAME TIME.

Our loving actions often speak louder than our words when others realize we're willing to go out of our way to help them. The apostle Paul wrote, "Though I am free and belong to no one, I have made myself a slave to everyone, to win as many as possible" (1 Corinthians 9:19).

People will wonder why you're willing to go the extra mile to serve them and meet their needs, and eventually they will ask you why. Then you will have the perfect opportunity to tell them. Remember the saying often attributed to St. Francis of Assisi: "Preach the Gospel, and if necessary, use words."

While our church always looks for ways to serve others, one of my favorite ways is what we call Serve Day. These designated days allow us to meet people where they are and to attend to their needs. On Serve Days we clean gutters and repair roofs, replace porches and mow yards. We mentor kids and tutor students, provide meals and repair cars—whatever we can do to serve people in the community. We show them the love of Jesus before we talk about it. We serve their needs and watch them open their hearts to God. And inevitably, those we serve ask us why we do it, and we tell them why.

CONNECT BEFORE YOU CORRECT

Jesus brought people together because he *connected* before he *corrected*. This was on display when he encountered Zacchaeus, a wealthy chief tax collector and known sinner. Let's revisit this story and consider how Jesus connected with Zacchaeus. Jesus was passing through Jericho, and apparently Zacchaeus was curious and wanted to see who Jesus was, perhaps wondering if the stories he'd heard about the carpenter from Nazareth were

> JESUS BROUGHT
> PEOPLE TOGETHER
> BECAUSE HE
> *CONNECTED*
> BEFORE HE
> *CORRECTED.*

true. The only problem, as you might have learned from a memorable Sunday school song, was that Zacchaeus was too short to see over the crowds: "a wee little man was he." So he climbed a sycamore-fig tree to watch Jesus pass by (Luke 19:1-4). Likely hoping to go unnoticed, the short man must have been surprised when Jesus stopped right below him, looked up, and said, "Zacchaeus, come down immediately. I must stay at your house today" (Luke 19:5).

Zacchaeus went down at once and welcomed him gladly, but the onlookers were not happy about it. They all began to mutter about how Jesus was going to be the guest of a sinner—had, in fact, invited himself to lunch with someone they all looked down on (Luke 19:7).

Jesus' willingness to eat a meal with Zacchaeus in his home made a strong connection. We're not told what they discussed or how their conversation unfolded, but the impact of their time together was undeniable. Zacchaeus emerged from their lunch declaring he would give half his possessions to the poor—and pay back what he had stolen from others four times over (Luke 19:8).

Jesus established a relational connection with someone

JESUS BROUGHT PEOPLE TOGETHER   177

most people despised before addressing the reason they likely despised Zacchaeus—his corruption, greed, and theft. "Today salvation has come to this house," Jesus announced, "because this man, too, is a son of Abraham" (Luke 19:9). In other words, Zacchaeus was no worse than those looking down on him; like them, he was a descendant of Abraham and just as worthy. As the ultimate high-road leader, Jesus connected with people first.

We have ample opportunities to follow Jesus' example today. We have the ability to make Christianity attractive to those around us, but too many Christians curse the darkness and complain about all that they see wrong with the world. God, however, has called us to turn on the light, to bring people not only together but to point them to God's love. We can reveal the truth and show grace at the same time. The Holy Spirit makes it possible for us to take the high road:

> But what happens when we live God's way? He brings gifts into our lives, much the same way that fruit appears in an orchard—things like *affection for others*, exuberance about life, *serenity*. We develop a willingness to stick with things, a sense of *compassion* in the heart, and a *conviction* that a basic holiness permeates things and people. We find ourselves involved in *loyal commitments*, not needing to force our way in life, able to *marshal and direct our energies* wisely." (Galatians 5:22-23, MSG, emphasis added)

Recent studies, including one by the Barna Group, reveal that a vast majority of people who develop a relationship with God do so after having a relationship with a Christian. We should want our lives to be so attractive that people want to know God because they know us. We are to be ambassadors for Jesus and walking advertisements for the gospel message. When we live and lead like Jesus, we cannot help but bring people together.

BLESSING PEOPLE TOGETHER

In order to convey the extravagance of God's love, we must love extravagantly. People are used to being treated in the same manner they treat others. This is the middle-road way of living and leading. It's the *quid-pro-quo* way of the world—you do something for me, and I'll do something for you. Jesus, however, turned this upside down and challenged believers to take the high road. Let's look again at what Jesus said in the Sermon on the Mount:

> You have heard that it was said, "Eye for eye, and tooth for tooth." But I tell you, do not resist an evil person. If anyone slaps you on the right cheek, turn to them the other cheek also. And if anyone wants to sue you and take your shirt, hand over your coat as well. If anyone forces you to go one mile, go with them two miles. (Matthew 5:38-41)

The Old Testament law, which Jesus referenced, communicated the prevailing attitude of fairness held by the Jews. The Romans felt strongly about retaliation. They worshipped the god of revenge, determined to get even with others by dishing out what they had received themselves. Jesus made it clear that treating others this way might be in line with human standards, but heavenly standards reflect the irrational extravagance of his Father's love.

We explored the idea of giving more than you take as a high-road principle in chapter 3. Jesus took that idea even further than simple generosity. He said, "You have heard that it was said, 'Love your neighbor and hate your enemy.' But I tell you: Love your enemies and pray for those who persecute you" (Matthew 5:43-44). Not only are we to give more than we take, but we are even called to love those intent on harming us. This counterintuitive command reflects the kind of divine *agape* love that comes only from God. We can never love our enemies unless we have experienced God's love personally. Once we have experienced it, God expects nothing less than for us to love our enemies.

As if this notion weren't already radical enough, Jesus then ramped it up even more. Not only did he ask us to go the extra mile and turn the other cheek, not only did he command us to love those who clearly do not love us—he asked us to bless them! Jesus said, "But to you who are listening I say: Love your enemies, do good to those who hate you, bless those who curse you, pray for those who mistreat you" (Luke 6:27-28).

What does it mean to bless someone? It means to speak well of them and want the best for them. Blessing is the opposite of cursing and means you refuse to gossip or spread falsehoods. Blessing someone not only means loving them but expressing this love with divine favor. Peter admonished, "Do not do wrong to repay a wrong, and do not insult to repay an insult. But repay with a blessing, because you yourselves were called to do this so that you might receive a blessing" (1 Peter 3:9, NCV). Rather than giving someone what we or they might think they deserve, love them and bless them. Why? Because this is how God has loved us.

SIX WAYS TO BRING PEOPLE TOGETHER

So many people separate and divide rather than bring together and bless. Jesus welcomes everyone and willingly extends his blessing to them, showing just how much he values them. He knows that words have power to bring people together. You and I can bring people together by following his example:

1.   Look for the Good in Every Person

The first way is simply by seeing the good in others and pointing it out. Proverbs says, "A word fitly spoken is like apples of gold in a setting of silver" (Proverbs 25:11, ESV). People are created in God's image, which means there is goodness in everyone. We can find it if we look for it, and we can let them know we see that goodness.

Jesus demonstrated this even while experiencing the agony of dying on the cross. While one thief next to Jesus mocked him, the other one pointed out, "We are punished justly, for we are getting what our deeds deserve. But this man has done nothing wrong. . . . Jesus, remember me when you come into your kingdom" (Luke 23:41-42). Jesus saw the good faith inside the man and responded, "Truly I tell you, today you will be with me in paradise" (Luke 23:43).

In addition to drawing others to you, praising the good qualities you see in people helps them to recognize their gifting and purpose. I've tried to do this with each of our kids. I identify their individual gifts and speak blessings over them. One of my children is very smart, while another is

SO MANY PEOPLE SEPARATE AND DIVIDE RATHER THAN BRING TOGETHER AND BLESS. JESUS WELCOMES EVERYONE AND WILLINGLY EXTENDS HIS BLESSING TO THEM, SHOWING JUST HOW MUCH HE VALUES THEM.

good with people. One child always spots beauty, while another loves to help others. My kids need me to see the best in them so they can know who they are and how God made them. I also try to do this with everyone I meet, and I encourage you to do the same.

2. Express Your Gratitude to Everyone

I have been very intentional about telling our kids, along with many others, how thankful I am for them. Every chance I get, I love saying, "You're a gift from God" or "I thank God for you." And it blesses me when someone shows me gratitude. Recently I was working in my office when my wife, Tammy, gently knocked and came in. She just wanted to let me know how much she loves me and thanks God for me. It was so encouraging.

Jesus frequently thanked his Father for providing both material items and spiritual power. Before blessing the loaves and fishes he would use to feed more than five thousand people, Jesus thanked God for the meager provision he used to perform a miracle (John 6:11). Before calling out his friend Lazarus from the tomb, Jesus thanked his Father for the ability to raise the dead (John 11:41). Jesus had an attitude of continual gratitude.

Giving thanks has the ability to bring people together because they feel seen, appreciated, and valued. Whenever I'm someone's guest or simply out in public, I've learned to say thank you and to show appreciation for our hosts and anyone who serves. If it positively impacts strangers and acquaintances, that is all the more reason to practice it with those who mean the most to us.

3.   Let Everyone Know How Much You Care

Showing and expressing affection demonstrates our attunement to others' needs and lets people know how much we care. Jesus never hesitated to touch someone to heal them, although he could have done it by merely willing it. Nor did he pull away from people. During the Last Supper, John, the disciple whom Jesus loved, rested his head on his Master's chest (John 13:25).

God the Father also expressed his affection for Jesus. On two remarkable occasions—Jesus' baptism by John and the transfiguration—God audibly spoke a blessing of love for his only Son. When Jesus came up from the water, "At that moment heaven was opened, and he saw the Spirit of God descending like a dove and alighting on him. And a voice from heaven said, 'This is my Son, whom I love; with him I am well pleased'" (Matthew 3:16-17). God communicated clearly with intimate affection by calling Jesus his Son and with overt affirmation by saying he was very pleased.

We should not assume others know how much we care about them. We must be willing to tell them directly and show them by how we interact with them.

4. Encourage Everyone You Meet

Encouragement is another powerful tool for bringing people together. Jesus' presence encouraged people by giving them hope. But he also spoke specific words of encouragement to people to lift them up. To Simon he said, "And I tell you that you are Peter, and on this rock I will build my church, and the gates of Hades will not overcome it" (Matthew 16:18). And after his death, burial, and resurrection, Jesus appeared to his disciples in the upper room where they had gathered to hide out from the Jewish authorities who might arrest them. He knew they were scared and anxious, and he greeted them with reassurance and encouragement, saying, "Peace be with you! As the Father has sent me, I am sending you" (John 20:21).

When we encourage others, we raise their courage to meet their need. Encouragement lets others know you can handle their discouragement and boost them when they need it most. You can identify someone's discouragement and flip it to bolster and strengthen them. As Paul said, "Do not let any unwholesome talk come out of your mouths, but only what is helpful for building others up according to their needs, that it may benefit those who listen" (Ephesians 4:29).

5. Show Kindness and Consideration in Every Situation

Kindness might seem like an obvious way to bring people

together, but you would be surprised how easy it is to overlook. Keep in mind, too, that kindness is not just being nice. Kindness is active and conveys safety, consideration, and compassion. You can see this in Jesus as our Good Shepherd, who pursues the one lost sheep that has wandered astray (Matthew 18:12-14).

Kindness, though gentle, is not weak or passive, but is intentional and powerful. The kindness modeled by Jesus indicated an attitude of grace

> KINDNESS IS ACTIVE AND CONVEYS SAFETY, CONSIDERATION, AND COMPASSION. YOU CAN SEE THIS IN JESUS AS OUR GOOD SHEPHERD, WHO PURSUES THE ONE LOST SHEEP THAT HAS WANDERED ASTRAY.

present in every interaction, an extravagant generosity of going above and beyond, and the compassion of empathizing with people's needs, such as a short man's curiosity or a sinful woman's shame. While anger and criticism divide and separate, kindness brings people together. That's why "a gentle answer turns away wrath, but a harsh word stirs up anger" (Proverbs 15:1).

6. Pray with and for Everyone You Can

The final way I suggest we bring people together is by praying with them and for them. Your willingness to talk to God about others shows how much you value them. And your heart gets right when you bring someone before the Father in prayer. It's hard not to love someone when you pray for them. Jesus prayed for children and blessed them (Matthew 19:13-15). He prayed for Simon's protection from Satan during the Last Supper (Luke 22:31-32). And he prayed for all his followers the night before he went to the cross (John 17:9-18).

Our words are so powerful in their ability to unite and bring together. As high-road leaders like Jesus, we are called to bless and not to curse, to attract and not to repel. When you go out of your way to show everyone God's love, display grace in how you interact with them, and bless them, you will bring people together. This is what it means to live out the gospel message, to represent Jesus in all your relationships.

THE ULTIMATE PLAN OF GOD

Why did Jesus always travel the high road? Why did he value all people, never keep score, give more than he took, acknowledge his humanness, do the right things for the right reasons, embrace authenticity, place people above his agenda, and bring people together? Because he wanted to bring all of us back to God. Sin created a chasm separating humankind from God, and Jesus bridged that gap through his death on the cross. Jesus paid the price for our sin and transgressions: "Once you were far away from God, but now you have been brought near to him through the blood of Christ" (Ephesians 2:13, NLT).

To be true followers of Christ, we must follow the path Jesus wants us to travel. We must act in the same way Jesus, the ultimate high-road leader, did. We are called to bring people together and to bring them to God. That has been his plan from the beginning. And it was Jesus himself who said, "Anyone who loves me will obey my teaching. My Father will love them, and we will come to them and make our home with them" (John 14:23).

It's relatively easy to exclude those who are different from us, to condemn those who don't share our beliefs and personal faith, and to overlook those outside our comfort zones. But that's not how Jesus acted. He *always* took the high road. He reached out to people who were different, engaged others with grace, and loved outsiders with compassionate connection.

We can do these things too. Jesus has set the example for us. God has given us the Holy Spirit, so we have the power to take the high road. And every day we receive the opportunity to make that choice. Which road will we take?

ABOUT THE AUTHORS

John C. Maxwell is a #1 *New York Times* bestselling author, speaker, coach, and leader who has sold more than 36 million books in fifty languages. He is the founder of Maxwell Leadership—the leadership development organization created to expand the reach of his principles of helping people lead powerful, positive change. Maxwell's books and programs have been translated into 70 languages and have been used to train tens of millions of leaders in every nation. His work also includes that of the Maxwell Leadership Foundation and EQUIP, nonprofit organizations that have impacted millions of adults and youth across the globe through values-based, people-centric leadership training.

John has been recognized as the #1 leader in business by the American Management Association and as the world's most influential leadership expert by both *Business Insider* and *Inc. Magazine*. He is a recipient of the Horatio Alger Award and the Mother Teresa Prize for Global Peace and Leadership from the Luminary Leadership Network.

Maxwell and the work of Maxwell Leadership continue to influence individuals and organizations worldwide—from Fortune 500 CEOs and national leaders to entrepreneurs and the leaders of tomorrow. For more information about him and Maxwell Leadership, visit maxwellleadership.com.

Chris Hodges is the founding and senior pastor of Church of the Highlands (churchofthehighlands. com) based in Birmingham, Alabama. Under his leadership, Church of the Highlands offers more than 75 worship services each weekend at 26 campuses/locations with 60,000-plus people attending weekly. Over its 23-year history, Church of the Highlands has given more than $144 million to charitable causes in Alabama and around the world, which would put Church of the Highlands on the Forbes 100 list of the largest charities in America.

Chris co-founded the Association of Related Churches (ARC) (arcchurches.com) in 2001, which trains more than 1,000 church planters every year. To date, ARC has helped start over 2000 new churches across the USA.

Chris also founded a coaching network called GrowLeader (GrowLeader.com) specializing in training and resourcing pastors and churches to help them break barriers and reach their growth potential. Each year more than 4,000 pastors and leaders attend sold-out conferences and roundtables in America, Europe, Australia, and Asia led by Chris and his team. These events equip pastors and leaders in a systematic model based on his bestselling books *What's Next?* and *Fresh Air*. GrowLeader currently serves more than 18,000 churches in at least 100 countries.

Chris is *New York Times* bestselling author, and his other books include *The Daniel Dilemma*, *Four Cups*, *Out of the Cave,* and his latest book, *Pray First: The Transformative Power of a Life Built on Prayer.*

Chris is also founder and Chancellor of Highlands College (highlandscollege.com), America's Ministry Leadership University, based in Birmingham, Alabama. Highlands College was founded in 2011 and prepares students who are called into vocational Christian ministry. As an innovative Bible college in the academy model, it focuses on a holistic four-pillar education of academic instruction, ministry training, character formation, and spiritual development. Its graduates serve and lead in churches and ministry organizations around the world.

Chris serves as Vice-Chairman on the Board of Directors of EQUIP (iequip.org), a global leadership training organization founded by John Maxwell. EQUIP has trained more than 6 million leaders in 196 countries of the world.

Chris also serves on the Board of Advisors of Global Teen Challenge (globaltc.org), a non-profit organization whose mission is to help men, women, boys, and girls in every nation find freedom from life-controlling addictions.

His educational background includes a BA in Management from Colorado Christian University and a Masters of Ministry from Southwestern Christian University.

Chris and his wife, Tammy, have five children and nine grandchildren and live in Birmingham, Alabama.

NOTES

[1] C. S. Lewis, *The Weight of Glory: And Other Addresses* (New York: Harper Collins, 2009), Kindle, 46 of 193.

[2] Samuel Johnson, *Oxford Essential Quotations,* 4th ed, Susan Ratcliffe, ed. (Oxford: Oxford University Press, 2016), https://www.oxfordreference.com/display/10.1093/acref/9780191826719.001.0001/q-oro-ed4-00005955#Q-ORO-0002465, accessed March 29, 2024.

[3] Beth M. Ley, *God Wants You Well!* (Detroit: BL Publications, 2001), 60-61.

[4] Max Lucado, "Prayer: A Heavenly Invitation," MaxLucado.com, https://maxlucado.com/prayer-a-heavenly-invitation/, accessed April 22, 2024.

[5] Kenn Filkins, "The Pit," *in Fearfully and Wonderfully Weird: A Screwball Look at the Church and Other Things*, complied by Doug Peterson and H. Winfield Tutte (Grand Rapids: The Door/Zondervan, 1990), 31.

[6] "Thoughts on the Business of Life," *Forbes,* February 1, 1949, 34.

[7] Ernest Hemingway, "The Capital of the World," *The Complete Short Stories of Ernest Hemingway*, Finca Vigía Edition (New York: Scribner, 2003), 29 of 652, Kindle.

[8]Martin Luther King Jr., "Draft of Chapter IV, 'Love in Action'" (sermon draft), The Martin Luther King, Jr. Research and Education Institute, Stanford University, https://kinginstitute.stanford.edu/king-papers/documents/draft-chapter-iv-love-action, accessed March 12, 2024.

[9] Mark Batterson, *Win the Day: 7 Daily Habits to Help You Stress Less and Accomplish More* (Colorado Springs: Multnomah, 2020), xii of 235, Kindle.

[10]Beau Bauman, ed., *The Most Important Thing I've Learned in Life* (New York: Fireside, 1994), 28.

[11] "Our Current Numbers," https://dlpcapital.com, accessed March 14, 2024.

[12] "Founder and CEO: Don Wenner," https://dlpcapital.com/about/team/don-wenner, accessed March 15, 2024.

[13] Bruce Wilkinson, *You Were Born for This: 7 Keys to a Life of Predictable Miracles* (Colorado Springs: Multnomah, 2009), 197.

[14] Lloyd John Ogilvie, *Let God Love You* (Waco: Word, 1974), 139-140.

[15]"Do Good Anyway: The Paradoxical Commandments," Quote Investigator, https://quoteinvestigator.com/2012/05/18/do-good-anyway/, May 18, 2012.

[16] Nancy Kennedy, *When He Doesn't Believe: Help and Encouragement for Women Who Feel Alone in Their Faith* (Colorado Springs: Waterbrook, 2001), 192.

[17] Charles Colson with Ellen Santilli Vaughn, *God and Government: An Insider's View on the Boundaries Between Faith and Politics* (Grand Rapids: Zondervan, 2007), 95.

[18] Henri J. M. Nouwen, *Out of Solitude: Three Meditations on the Christian Life* (Notre Dame: Ave Maria Press, 2004), 55 of 65, Kindle.

[19] Eugene B. Habecker, *The Other Side of Leadership* (Wheaton, IL: Victor Books, 1987), 217.

[20] Mrs. C. R. Klein, "Entrance Exam," *The Reader's Digest,* Volume 74 (1959), 152.

[21] Joseph Sutton, ed., *Words of Wellness: A Treasury of Quotations for Well-Being* (Carlsbad, CA: Hay House, 1991), 2145 of 3667, Kindle.